D1561983

THE MONETARY POLICY
OF FOURTEENTH-CENTURY FLORENCE

Published under the auspices of the
Center for Medieval and Renaissance Studies
University of California, Los Angeles

Publications of the

UCLA CENTER FOR MEDIEVAL AND RENAISSANCE STUDIES

1. Jeffrey Burton Russell, *Dissent and Reform in the Early Middle Ages* (1965)
2. C. D. O'Malley, ed., *Leonardo's Legacy: An International Symposium* (1968)
3. Richard H. Rouse, *Guide to Serial Bibliographies for Medieval Studies* (1969)
4. Speros Vryonis, Jr., *The Decline of Medieval Hellenism in Asia Minor and the Process of Islamization from the Eleventh through the Fifteenth Century* (1971)
5. Stanley Chodorow, *Christian Political Theory and Church Politics in the Mid-Twelfth Century: The Ecclesiology of Gratian's Decretum* (1972)
6. Joseph J. Duggan, *The Song of Roland: Formulaic Style and Poetic Craft* (1973)
7. Ernest A. Moody, *Studies in Medieval Philosophy, Science, and Logic: Collected Papers 1933–1969* (1975)
8. Marc Bloch, *Slavery and Serfdom in the Middle Ages: Selected Essays* (1975)
9. Michael J. B. Allen, *Marsilio Ficino: The Philebus Commentary, A Critical Edition and Translation* (1975)
10. Richard C. Dales, *Marius: On the Elements, A Critical Edition and Translation* (1976)
11. Duane J. Osheim, *An Italian Lordship: The Bishopric of Lucca in the Late Middle Ages* (1977)
12. Robert Somerville, *Pope Alexander III and the Council of Tours (1163): A Study of Ecclesiastical Politics and Institutions in the Twelfth Century* (1977)
13. Lynn White, Jr., *Medieval Religion and Technology: Collected Essays* (1978)
14. Michael J. B. Allen, *Marsilio Ficino and the Phaedran Charioteer: Introduction, Texts, Translations* (1981)
15. Barnabas Bernard Hughes, O.F.M., *Jordanus de Nemore: De numeris datis, A Critical Edition and Translation* (1981)
16. Caroline Walker Bynum, *Jesus as Mother: Studies in the Spirituality of the High Middle Ages* (1982)
17. Cipolla, Carlo, *The Monetary Policy of Fourteenth-Century Florence* (1983).

CARLO M. CIPOLLA

The Monetary Policy of Fourteenth-Century Florence

University of California Press

Berkeley • Los Angeles • London

The emblem of the Center
for Medieval and Renaissance Studies
reproduces the imperial eagle of
the gold *augustalis* struck
after 1231 by Emperor Frederick II;
Elvira and Vladimir Clain-Stefanelli,
The Beauty and Lore of Coins, Currency and Medals
(Croton-on-Hudson, 1974), fig. 130 and p. 106.

University of California Press
Berkeley and Los Angeles, California
University of California Press, Ltd.,
London, England
Copyright (c) 1982 by
The Regents of the University of California
ISBN 0-520-04606-4
Printed in the United States of America
1 2 3 4 5 6 7 8 9

Library of Congress Cataloging in Publication Data

Cipolla, Carlo M.
The monetary policy of fourteenth-century Florence.

Bibliography: p. Includes index. 1. Monetary
policy—Italy—Florence—History—14th .fl century.
2. Money—Italy—Florence—History—14th century.
3. Coinage—Italy—Florence—History—14th
century. I. Title.
HG1040.F55C56
1982   332.4'94551   82-13358
ISBN 0-520-04606-4

Contents

Preface

THE AIM of this little book is to portray the working of the monetary system and the nature of monetary policy in a medieval city-state. The case chosen is fourteenth-century Florence and the reasons for the choice are not difficult to explain. First, for fourteenth-century Florence there is available a rich documentation that can hardly be found for any other medieval city-state. Second, Florence was at that time the most important financial center of Western Europe. Third, the fourteenth century was in Florence a time of dramatic events, such as the great crash of the 1340s and the Ciompi revolt of 1378. Uncomfortable as such events may have been for the people of the time, they add interest to a study aimed at observing the interplay between economic conditions, social and political situations, and monetary policies and developments.

Politically and administratively Florence was a city-state organized in the form of a Commune, that is, a self-governing association of free citizens which was the product of two centuries of historical evolution.

From a legalistic point of view, the Commune was not a completely sovereign entity, for in theory it recognized the supreme authority of a distant emperor. In practice it performed as a sovereign entity, although its sovereignty was by modern standards severely limited by bodies such as the Church and the Guilds, which possessed various degrees of independence with corresponding privileges, immunities, and separate jurisdictional powers.

The monetary system of Florence was based on gold and silver coins. The gold coin, the florin, was a piece of pure gold that weighed approximately 3.53 grams. The silver coins were divided into two groups: the *moneta grossa*, represented by the *grosso* (groat), made of good silver alloy (953/1000), and the *moneta piccola*, represented by petty coins made of base alloy, that is, an alloy that contained much copper and little silver: these petty coins were the *denaro picciolo* (penny) and the *quattrino* (fourpence). This system was the result of a long story that can be briefly summarized as follows.

The monetary systems of the various states of medieval Italy had their origin in the reforms enacted by Charlemagne sometime between 781 and 794. At that time the king of the Franks generalized a monetary system for his dominions in France, Germany, and Italy that was as simple as it was crude: in its final form this system was based on a single silver coin called *denarius* (penny), weighing about 1.7 grams of silver of about 950/1000 fineness. The penny had neither multiples nor submultiples. People had to invent abstract multiples in order to avoid using numbers too large to handle; they used the term *libra* (pound) to indicate 240 *denari* and the term *solidus* (shilling) for 12 *denari*.[1] The roughness and simplicity of the system reflected the extremely primitive nature of the economy, where exchanges and the use of money were reduced to a bare minimum.

With the tenth century and more definitively with the eleventh and twelfth centuries, the situation changed: the population grew, production and trade increased, and the use of money became more widespread. At the same time, the *denaro* was gradually reduced in both weight and fineness. Furthermore, there arose as many new mints as there were states and principalities on the ruins of the empire. These different trends were correlated, but they also contained elements of internal contradiction.

In my opinion, the debasement of the *denaro* was not a bad thing. Given the relatively inelastic supply of silver and the lack of an adequate expansion of credit, in the face of a growing demand for money, the debasement of the *denaro* prevented deflationary pressures from developing and hampering the process of economic growth. However, the sacrifice of the *denaro* was not the outcome of a conscious and logically thought out monetary policy. It was more the spontaneous and uncontrolled result of market pressures and empirical reactions.

After the middle of the twelfth century, the *denaro* from any mint in Northern Italy had been reduced in size and appearance to a totally wretched and ugly little disk of metal, very thin, of low fineness, easy to

---

[1]*Libra* was the latin name of the pound weight (about 410 grams). *Solidus* was the name of an ancient coin against which the *denarius* was eventually valued in the ratio of 12 to 1.

lose, and easy to break. At the domestic level, there was increasingly felt a need for a system with more denominations—that is, a system with multiples and submultiples. At the international level, the need was increasingly felt for a sound means of payment with high unitary value that would be stable in its metallic content. In response to these needs, the *grosso* appeared between the end of the twelfth century and the beginning of the thirteenth. The following data provide some information about the mintings of early *grossi* in the various Italian cities.[2]

It should be borne in mind that the table reflects only developments in Italy. *Grossi* were soon coined

City	Date	Value of *grosso* (in local *denari*)	Weight (in grams)
Genoa	end of 12th century	4	1.4
Genoa	end of 12th century	6	1.7
Venice	c. 1202	26	2.2
Siena	1220/1230	12	1.7
Pisa	1227 (?)	12	1.7
Verona	c. 1230	20	1.7
Parma	c. 1230	4	1.7
Bologna	before 1233	12	1.5
Ferrara	before 1233	12	1.5
Reggio	1233	12	1.5
Florence	1230/1240	12	1.7

[2]P. H. Grierson, "The Origins of the Grosso and of Gold Coinage in Italy," *Numismaticky Sbornik* 12 (1971–1972), p. 34. Cf. also D. Herlihy, "Pisan Coinage and the Monetary History of Tuscany, 1150–1250," in *Le Zecche minori toscane fino al XIV secolo* (Pistoia, 1967).

outside Italy as well, and the Venetian *grosso* rapidly enjoyed great popularity in the Levant, where it became a commonly accepted means of payment.

Until the beginning of the thirteenth century, Florence was only indirectly involved in these developments. It did not mint its own money, and the Florentines used currency from Lucca and later from Pisa. Florence entered the monetary scene when the first *grossi* were coined in Tuscany, and it came to the forefront in 1252. In that year the Florentines carried the motives underlying the introduction of the *grosso* to their ultimate conclusion: taking advantage of a fall in the value of gold in relation to silver, they coined the gold florin.

The coining of the gold florin was such an important event in the monetary history of the Occident that it deserves closer scrutiny. During the early Middle Ages, gold currency had been minted in Southern Italy in the form of the gold *tarì*, which was the successor of the Arabian quarter *dinar (rubā'i)* of the Aghlabids and Fatimids. In 1231, the year of the publication of the Constitutions of Melfi, Frederick II issued a gold coin called the *augustale*, weighing 5.28 grams, with a fineness of 20.5 carats and worth 7–1/2 *tarì* of account. In a sense, the *augustale* continued the tradition of South Italian gold coinage. But in other respects—that is, its decidedly classical design and its characteristics of fineness and weight—the *augustale* represented an innovation, foreshadowing the monetary revolution that would take place twenty years later, in 1252.

In the broad picture of Western coinage, the gold currency of Southern Italy from the ninth to twelfth centuries represents, with the gold coinage of Moslem Spain, an anomalous occurrence—proving (were it ever

necessary) that Southern Italy in those centuries belonged more to the Byzantine and Moslem economic
areas than to the Western world. The Christian West
since the Carolingian monetary reforms had remained
strictly anchored to silver monometallism. With the development of exchanges and production after the tenth
century, gold currency came to be used in the more
important centers of the West, but the gold currency
used was Byzantine, Moslem, and South Italian. However, in 1252, twenty-one years after the appearance of
Frederick II's *augustale*, the republic of Genoa issued a
coin of pure gold, weighing about 3.52 grams and called
the *genovino d'oro*. In November of the same year, Florence issued a coin of pure gold, weighing about 3.53
grams and called the *fiorino d'oro*. Venice moved cau-
tiously and was slow to follow the Genoese and Florentine examples. The caution was dictated by the success
and popularity of the Venetian silver *grosso* in the Levantine markets, and by the desire not to create a need-
less competitor to its own well-established currency. But
after a few decades Venice decided to follow the Genoese and Florentine example. In October 1284 the government of the Venetian Republic ordered the minting of a
coin called the *ducato d'oro*; it too was of pure gold and
weighed 3.56 grams. The monometallism inaugurated
by Charlemagne four-and-a-half centuries earlier thus
came to a decisive close in Western Europe.[3]

In the ordinance of October 1284, whereby the Venetian High Council ordered the minting of the gold ducat, the currency taken as standard was not the *genovino* of Genoa but the florin of Florence: "capta fuit

[3]Cf. R. S. Lopez, *Settecento anni fa: il ritorno all'oro nell'Occidente
Duecentesco* (Naples, 1955). Translated and condensed in "Back to
Gold, 1252," *The Economic History Review*, ser. 2, vol. 9 (1956).

pars quod debeat laborari moneta auri communis vi-
delicet LXVII pro marcha auri tam bona et fina per
aurum vel melior ut est florenus."[4] Venice was not the
only city to refer to the florin as a model. As time
passed, various European mints began to strike currency that imitated the Florentine florin in weight, fineness, and often even in design. Indeed, between the
middle of the thirteenth century and the beginning of
the fourteenth, the Florentine gold florin established
itself as the dominant international currency in conti-
nental Europe. The total revenues of the Apostolic
Chamber during the pontificate of Pope John XXII
(1316–1334) consisted of more than three and a half
million gold florins, as opposed to only 272,259 gold
agneaux of France, 149,425 doubloons, 3,237 Venetian
ducats, 346 gold *genovini*, and other currencies of little
importance.[5] One might suggest that these proportions
were influenced by the fact that at that time the Florentines were the Pope's bankers. But private treasures
confirm the enormous preponderance of the florin
among the gold coins circulating in Western Europe: a
private hoard dating from about 1340, discovered in
Limburg an der Lahn in Germany in 1957, is typical in
this respect. It consisted of 126 gold coins: 84 Florentine florins, 26 imitations of the florin, 9 French *écus*, 6
imitations of the *écu*, and 1 Venetian ducat.

If analogous information were available for the coins
circulating in the Middle East, it is almost certain the
Venetian ducat would be found to have held a privi-

[4]A photographic reproduction of the document can be found in
C. Cipolla, *Money, Prices, and Civilization in the Mediterranean World*
(Princeton, 1956), fig. 2.

[5]E. Göller, *Die Einnahmen der Apostolischen Kammer unter Johann
XII*, Vatikanische Quellen (Paderborn, 1910), pp. 15–16.

leged position there with respect to the Florentine
florin. But it remains true that in Europe the florin
played the predominant role.[6] Its prestige and position
were based on its intrinsic stability and on the power
that the Florentine bankers had acquired in the system
of exchanges and as financial intermediaries in Europe
of the time.

In the course of the following pages the reader will
repeatedly encounter reference to Table D of the Appendix. It may be useful to provide the reader here with the
information that Table D can be found on p. 97.

While writing this book I incurred many debts. First
I should mention Mario Bernocchi and C. M. de la
Roncière. Without their earlier massive research and
monumental publication of data, this work would have
been impossible. I not only availed myself of their
books, but also exploited the authors in person, asking
for advice and more information. I also pestered R.
Barducci, A. Borlandi, G. Brucker, M. Casini, A. Cas-
tellani, G. Pallanti, G. Pansini, G. Pinto, J. M. Smith,
L. S. Yang. and, last but not least, my wife, Ora. Professor M. de Cecco read an early draft of the first
chapter and made valuable suggestions. To all these
people I wish to express my gratitude. My thanks are
also due to Muriel Kittel, who translated the original
Italian text into the English language, to the Institute of
International Studies of the University of California at
Berkeley, and Mrs. Peggy Nelson, and Mrs. Susan
Reisner for their help in preparing the typescript.

[6]P. Berghaus, "Umlauf und Nachprägung des Florentiner Guldens Nördlich des Alpen," in *Atti del Congresso internazionale di numismatica, Roma, 11–16 settembre 1961* (Rome, 1965), pp. 595–607; J. B.
Giard, *Le florin d'or au Baptiste et ses imitations en France au XIVe siecle*,
Bibliothèque de l'École des Chartes, 125 (Paris, 1967), pp. 94ff.

CHAPTER I

The Great Crash of 1343–1346

I

THE FIRST decades of the fourteenth century in Europe saw the end of a secular period of growth and the beginning of a long and arduous search for new equilibriums. A whole body of literature deals with the early *Trecento* and the related contrast between the vigorous expansion of the twelfth and thirteenth centuries and the difficult years of the fourteenth. The ultimate causes and some particular aspects of the change can be discussed indefinitely, but the fundamental outlines of the picture are clear and abundant evidence indicates that the change was not only economic and demographic, but also political, social, and cultural. The age of "The Canticle of the Sun" gave way to the age of the *Danse macabre*.

The economic history of Florence closely reflected Western developments. Florence grew dramatically in the course of the thirteenth century, and by the end of that century it had come to represent to the world of the time what London was to the nineteenth century: not only a great cultural, commercial, and manufacturing center, but also the principal financial market of the period. With the beginning of the fourteenth century, however, the fortunes of the city underwent a painful change.

The darkest years of the Florentine economy were those between 1339 and 1349. Long-run and short-run adverse factors of both local and international character combined to create a dramatic scenario. There was the bankruptcy of the Commune of Florence in 1345. There were the failures of the major banking and merchant houses between 1343 and 1346. There were the wild fluctuations in the relative values of gold and silver in the years 1345–1347 that threw the monetary system into confusion. There was the great famine of 1347, followed by the terrifying plague of 1348. Economic distress bred social tension and political upheaval: there was the Bardi conspiracy (1340), there was the desperate search for solutions to the various problems by submitting to a strong man in the person of Walter of Brienne (1342); there was the failure of the autocratic experiment and the expulsion of the tyrant (1343).

The various events interacted with one another in a complex way that cannot adequately be described in words. The scenario has to be broken up and its separate components analyzed one by one, with the obvious disadvantage of creating in the reader the false impression of linear causality, when in reality there were multiple and complicated reciprocal relationships.

Let us begin with the breakdown of public finance. At the beginning of the fourteenth century, the situation was still under control, with a public debt in the neighborhood of 50,000 gold florins.[1] The situation got out of hand because of the wars with which Florence was involved largely as a result of her previous economic expansion. Wars had come to be fought less and less by citizens and more and more by mercenary bands[2] and as a result required sums of money vastly in excess of the traditional sources of public revenue. At the close of the war against the Scaligers of Verona (1336–1338), the Commune of Florence was in debt for about 450,000 gold florins,[3] and the following war against Lucca (1341–1343) brought the outstanding debt to more than 600,000 gold florins.[4] This frightening increase in the public debt in less than a decade was the more serious in that the deterioration of the economic situation was reducing revenues.[5] Confronted by an increasingly precarious position, on November 20, 1342, Walter of Brienne, then Lord of Florence, suspended all allocations of customs revenue that were granted to the creditors of the Commune as the traditional means of recovering loaned capital and related

[1]B. Barbadoro, *Le finanze della Repubblica fiorentina* (Florence, 1929), p. 507.

[2]The employment of mercenary companies became prevalent in the first decades of the fourteenth century. Cf. D. P. Waley, "The Army of the Florentine Republic," in *Florentine Studies: Politics and Society in Renaissance Florence*, N. Rubinstein, ed. (Evanston, 1968), p. 106.

[3]A. Sapori, *La crisi delle compagnie mercantili dei Bardi e dei Peruzzi* (Florence, 1926), p. 114; R. Barducci, "Politica e speculazione finanziaria a Firenze dopo la crisi del primo Trecento (1343–1358)," *Archivio storico italiano* 137 (1979), p. 185.

[4]M. Villani, *Cronica*, F. Dragomanni, ed. (Florence, 1844–1845), III, 106; Barbadoro, *Le finanze*, p. 616; Barducci, "Politica e speculazione," p. 187, n. 49.

[5]Barducci, "Politica e speculazione," p. 186, n. 41.

interest.[6] About two years later, on February 22, 1345 (when Walter had been expelled for about two years), the Commune was forced to declare its inability to satisfy its creditors in the immediate future ('non est ad presens possibile restituere predictis creditoribus ea que recipere debent'); and on the debts, declared bad for the time being, it assigned a reduced interest of five percent.[7] Meanwhile, for reasons we shall go into later, shares in the public debt that were hitherto not transferable were declared negotiable.[8] However, both doubts as to their redemption and the lowering of the interest paid on them caused their market value to collapse.[9] The effect was comparable to that of a collapse of the stock exchange in our times. Almost all sections of society were affected, because most people, the wealthy as well as the not so wealthy, had made loans to the Commune.[10]

[6]Barbadoro, *Le finanze*, p. 623.

[7]Barbadoro, *Le finanze*, p. 644. However, Barbadoro's assertion that the provision of February 22, 1345, "transformed the old loans into a claim for perpetual income" is not correct. The Commune suspended reimbursements temporarily, with the intention of resuming them as soon as possible—which in fact was done by various ingenious financial devices only a few years after the declaration of 1345 (cf. Barducci, "Politica e speculazione," pp. 179ff.).

[8]Barbadoro, *Le finanze*, p. 645, n. 1. The declaration of the negotiability of shares took place on October 25, 1344, and was confirmed on February 22, 1345.

[9]Barducci, "Politica e speculazione," pp. 118, n. 57 and 190. Cf. also A. Sapori, "Pigioni di case e botteghe a Firenze nel Trecento," in *Studi di storia economica* (Florence, 1955), p. 331; A. Sapori, "L'interesse del denaro a Firenze," in *Studi di storia economica* (Florence, 1955), p. 238.

[10]Barbadoro, *Le finanze*, pp. 604–605. One has to consider that "loans" to the Commune were also forced on the population as an alternative to taxation.

Especially hard hit were the great families of the Florentine financial oligarchy.[11] During the euphoria of the preceding decades, the merchant and banking houses had willingly advanced the Commune substantial amounts of money, because they regarded the operation as a perfectly secure investment yielding good return. Now, between 1342 and 1345, they had to face a very different reality: the yield had collapsed and the soundness of credit had become doubtful.

In normal times most of the companies would have been able to ride out the storm. But the times were definitely not normal, and the Commune's bankruptcy hit the companies at the very moment when most of them were in a serious crisis of solvency.

At this point we must turn from public finance and focus on the private sector. The situation had already begun to deteriorate in the first years of the 1330s, and the profits of the greater companies had been diminishing.[12] In 1339, the situation, already serious, was aggravated by a famine, and the chronicler G. Villani reported that "every trade in Florence was in too poor a shape to make a profit."[13] But this was only the beginning of a series of far worse misfortunes. The truce of Esplechin (September 23, 1340) confirmed the failure of the expeditions with which Edward III of England had begun the protracted conflict with France that was to become known as the Hundred Years' War. It

[11]Barbadoro, Le finanze, pp. 495–496, 535, 560, 582, 589n. On December 20, 1345, the judges appointed for the bankruptcies called the public administration's attention to the fact that the companies in state of default were creditors of the Commune for "quam plures summas et quantitates pecunie" (Sapori, La crisi, p. 162).

[12]Sapori, La crisi, pp. 105–106.

[13]G. Villani, Cronica XI, 100.

became immediately apparent that the English king would not be in a position to repay what he owed the Florentine bankers who had subsidized his campaign. Involved in the gamble were two of the major houses of Florence, the Bardi and the Peruzzi, the Bardi's bank alone having advanced a sum of between 600,000 and 900,000 gold florins.[14]

Meanwhile, the results of the war fought by Florence in Lombardy stimulated a new struggle for the possession of the city of Lucca. In the feverish diplomatic game that accompanied this new war, Florence at one point gave the impression of being ready to leave its traditional Guelf allies and go over to the Ghibelline camp. The Florentine diplomatic moves alarmed Roberto, king of Naples, his barons, and the prelates of his kingdom—all of whom had deposited large sums of capital with Florentine bankers. The fear that their funds might be frozen drove them to make a rush of withdrawals that left the Florentine banks in big trouble.[15]

The paradigms that may help explain the English and Neapolitan events presuppose that the reader realizes that, at the beginning of the fourteenth century, Florence represented a developed and dominant economy, whereas both England and Naples were decidedly underdeveloped "periphery."

[14]The chronicler G. Villani reported that the king of England owed 900,000 gold florins to the Bardi and 600,000 to the Peruzzi. Sapori (*La crisi*, p. 77), after studying the extant accounts, concludes that one can "estimate the English king's debt to the Bardi's bank at an amount somewhere between 535,000 and 900,000 gold florins." But in a later study, A. Sapori ("Le compagnie italiane in Inghilterra," in *Studi di storia economica* [Florence, 1955], p. 1049) raised the lower estimate to 594,176 florins.

[15]G. Villani, *Cronica* XI, 138; Sapori, *La crisi*, p. 145.

In an over-simplified version, the paradigm applicable to the English royal bankruptcy may run as follows: the large companies of the dominant economy (Florence), which operate in the under-developed country (England), have a vital interest in securing the local raw material (wool) for the home market. By the logic of events they are led to grant increasingly larger credits to the local rulers, on whose benevolence the licenses for the export of raw material ultimately depend. The rulers of the underdeveloped country, however, instead of using the credit to finance productive investment, squander the funds in war expenses and are soon forced to declare bankruptcy.[16]

The paradigm applicable to the Neapolitan withdrawals is somewhat analogous. The large companies of the dominant economy (Florence), once established in the underdeveloped country (Naples) from which they import raw materials (grains, wool, cotton),[17] develop relations with the local aristocracy and collect its savings. The underdeveloped country's surplus is thus reexported as financial capital and accumulates in the

[16]Of course reality was more complex than the model. The Tuscan bankers made loans not only to the king but also to private individuals and ecclesiastical establishments that used the credit for productive purposes. Also, Englishmen sometimes deposited funds with the Tuscans. On this subject, see M. Prestwich, "Italian Merchants in Late Thirteenth and Early Fourteenth Century England," in *The Dawn of Modern Banking*, F. Chiapelli, ed. (New Haven and London, 1979), and the bibliography quoted therein. On the role of wool in the relationship between the Florentine houses and the English crown, cf. R. A. Goldthwaite, "Italian Bankers in Medieval England," *The Journal of European Economic History* 2 (1973), pp. 767ff.

[17]On the commercial and financial relationships between Florence and Southern Italy, see D. Abulafia, "Southern Italy and the Florentine Economy: 1265–1370," *The Economic History Review*, ser. 2, vol. 34 (1981).

form of deposits in the banks of the dominant economy, to be recycled. Short-term investment, however, is by its nature extremely volatile, and any kind of political turbulence can lead to an immediate recall of funds and cause a crisis in the banking system of the dominant economy.

The two paradigms are not alien to us. They could be applied to the events of the 1970s simply by altering the names of the chief actors and changing the kind of raw material involved. However, this is not the place to speculate on "distant mirrors" and indulge in parallels that, if pushed too far, would turn out to be anachronistic. Let us keep to the thread of events.

The triple blow of the English bankruptcy, the Neapolitan withdrawals, and the bankruptcy of the Commune was more than the Florentine banking system could bear. The grim signs of a crisis of exceptional magnitude daily became more evident and more threatening. Already on October 26, 1342, Walter of Brienne had to grant a three-year moratorium to the company of Taddeo dell'Antella, but it seems that all other financially embarrassed companies were allowed to take advantage of the same provision.[18] However, moratoriums do not solve financial crises. Ruin inevitably followed. After trying laboriously for some years to meet increasingly difficult conditions, the Peruzzi failed in 1343, and, three years later, in 1346, the Bardi failed.[19] The consequences were catastrophic. The two companies, particularly the Bardi, were among the greatest in Florence and therefore in the contemporary

[18]Sapori, *La crisi*, p. 148; Barbadoro, *Le finanze*, p. 623, n. 2.

[19]Sapori, *La crisi*, pp. 158–182.

world: two "pillars" of the economic system as the chronicler G. Villani defined them.[20]

In such cases one bankruptcy triggers another, and so, after the fall of the Peruzzi and the Bardi, the Acciaiuoli, the Bonaccorsi, the Cocchi, the Antellesi, the Corsini, the da Uzzano, and the Perendoli all went down.[21]

The collapse of the banks brought losses to all who held deposits in them; in the more fortunate instances depositors were indeed able to retrieve only a half, or a third, or a fifth of their funds.[22] The list of the Antellesis' creditors shows that among the depositors affected by the bank's collapse were people of all social classes and groups: magnates, as well as artisans, widows, and orphans.[23] A considerable mass of wealth was thus destroyed: "hardly any substance was left among our citizens," was Villani's bitter comment.[24]

Nor was this all. The collapse of the banks triggered the ruin of people and companies in other sectors both directly and indirectly—directly, because the great companies carried on mercantile and manufacturing activities in addition to their banking ones; indirectly, because the banks' failure caused a drastic shortage of credit. Actually, once the crisis had started, a perverse multiplier effect was set in motion by which the crisis

[20]G. Villani, Cronica XI, 88.

[21]G. Villani, Cronica XII, 55.

[22]G. Villani, Cronica XII, 55.

[23]A. Sapori, "Il quaderno dei creditori di Taddeo dell'Antella e Compagni," Rivista delle Biblioteche e degli Archivi, n.s. 3 (1925), pp. 168ff.; G. A. Brucker, Florentine Politics and Society (1343–1378) (Princeton, 1962), p. 17.

[24]G. Villani, Cronica XII, 55.

fed upon itself and spread like an oil stain. It should be made clear at this point that the sequence I am describing is not the product of theoretical speculation, but is plainly set out by the chronicler Giovanni Villani in terms that are strikingly similar to those used by present-day economists. Villani used the expression "mancamento della credenza,"[25] which literally translates into "want of credit," and the term "*rimbalzo*"[26] (which can be literally rendered with "rebound") to express what we mean by "the multiplier effect." According to his precise testimony, the failure of the companies was followed by a severe "want of credit," which, compounded by the effects of the "*rimbalzo*," caused a series of failures in a chain reaction that affected every section of the economy: "trade and all crafts declined and fell into a very bad state," and also "the small companies and individual craftsmen went bankrupt."[27]

Villani's testimony is confirmed by other chroniclers[28] and by the findings of modern historians. Catalogued among the archival records of communal elections, G. Brucker has found a list of 350 Florentines who suffered bankruptcy between 1333 and 1346, and the list is far from complete. At any rate, in addition to the prominent families—Bardi, Peruzzi, Acciaiuoli, Baroncelli, Antellesi—the list contains hundreds of unfamiliar names belonging to obscure, petty entrepreneurs.[29]

[25]G. Villani, *Cronica* XI, 88.

[26]G. Villani, *Cronica* XI, 88.

[27]G. Villani, *Cronica* XI, 88 and XII, 55.

[28]See Lionardo Aretino, *Dell'Historia Fiorentina*, Venice 1561, p. 135 v.

[29]Brucker, *Florentine Politics*, pp. 16–17.

A letter written in September 1344 by two Florentine businessmen to friends in France confirms the gravity of the economic situation and bears witness to the mood prevailing among the people: "the city of Florence today is in such a poor state for artisans and the lower classes that we can earn nothing."[30] The consequences of the crisis on the levels of employment caused unrest among the mass of the population.[31] In the face of such dramatic social and economic breakdown, Giovanni Villani commented: "our republic has lost all its power and our citizens have nearly all been impoverished. . . . For the city of Florence the ruin has been greater than had ever before fallen on our Commune."[32]

But the tribulations did not end there. After the English and the Neapolitans, the Florentines had to cope with acts of God. It had begun to rain in October 1345, and it did not stop. Torrential rains ruined the spring sowing. As a result, the 1346 harvest was pitiful and, according to the chronicler, the worst of the previous hundred years. There followed one of the most severe famines that Florence had ever experienced.[33]

In this desperate situation, the city managers resorted to every possible external source of supply, im-

[30]M. Becker and G. Brucker, "Una lettera in difesa della dittatura nella Firenze del Trecento," *Archivio storico italiano* 113 (1955), p. 258.

[31]N. Rodolico, *Il popolo minuto* (Bologna, 1889), doc. 19; Becker and Brucker, "Una lettera," p. 256. The level of unemployment in Florence must already have been high before the expulsion of Walter of Brienne (1343), because the latter initiated a building program to provide work for the unemployed. Cf. Paoli, "Della Signoria di Gualtieri," *Giornale storico degli archivi toscani* 6 (1862), pp. 30–32.

[32]G. Villani, *Cronica* XII, 55.

[33]For the whole story cf. G. Villani, *Cronica* XII, 73, and G. Pinto, *Il libro del Biadaiolo: carestie e annona a Firenze dalla metà del Duecento al 1348* (Florence, 1978), pp. 97–100.

porting grain however and from wherever they could. This imposed considerable extra strain on the Commune's already crumbling finances and compelled the city to export hard currency to the tune of 30,000 gold florins in 1347, in order to import grain from overseas markets.[34]

II

If we put together the pieces of the mosaic that have been gathered thus far, we may try to define the nature and character of the crisis. Between 1342 and 1345, the reader will recall, the public finance of Florence collapsed. The declaration (1345) of a temporary suspension of reimbursements and the setting of a maximum interest rate of 5 percent on the public debt must have caused a considerable reduction of liquidity on the market. The move to make the shares in the public debt negotiable (October 1344–February 1345) was a skillful one. It obviously aimed at increasing the level of liquidity in the market by making assets liquid that were not so before. Unfortunately the declaration of the negotiability of the shares was not enough to compensate for the negative effects of suspending reimbursements and limiting interest. The quotation of the shares fell to one third and less of their face value, and a substantial amount of financial wealth was thus lost. In the meantime, the banking houses failed (1343–1346), and more wealth was lost in the form of deposits that were either not reimbursed or only partially so.

[34]G. Villani, *Cronica* XII, 73; Pinto, *Il libro del Biadaiolo*, p. 121.

Giovanni Villani's comment has already been evoked: "hardly any substance was left among our citizens."[35]

The effects of this destruction of wealth were aggravated by another circumstance. The banks of that time had already developed to the point of creating money besides increasing its velocity of circulation.[36] Consequently, the banks' failure caused both a contraction of the quantity of money and a reduction of its velocity. We have no way of measuring the phenomenon, but there are no doubts as to its existence. Logical induction is supported by the explicit testimonial of the chronicler: "because of the said failures of the companies ready money was lacking and hardly to be found."[37]

A most serious deflationary pressure resulted. For those with ready cash, golden opportunities opened up, and Villani recorded: "some artisans and moneylenders with their usury swallow up and gather unto themselves the scattered poverty of our citizens and country people."[38] But for every hundred people forced to sell there was only one in a position to buy, and it was in fact almost impossible to find buyers. The collapse of the market for shares in the public debt has already been noted. More telling still was the collapse of real estate values. Here too, what might be logically deduced is explicit testified to by the contemporary chronicler: "he who wanted to sell properties in the city had to give for one what was worth two and yet no

[35]G. Villani, *Cronica* XII, 55.

[36]See R. C. Mueller, "The Role of Bank Money in Venice, 1300–1500," *Studi veneziani*, n.s., 3 (1979) and bibliography thereof.

[37]G. Villani, *Cronica* XI, 138.

[38]G. Villani, *Cronica* XII, 55.

buyer was to be found; and in the country at one third less of the value, and values dropped even further."[39] In other words, prices of real estate in the city fell by about 50 percent and in the country properties fell by about one-third, and still "no buyer was to be found."

The drop in property values was paralleled by falling rents. Information on this subject is rather scarce, but the documentation tracked down by Professor Armando Sapori for a limited number of shops in Florence allows us to glimpse a reduction in rents of approximately 25 percent between 1339 and 1345.[40] Wages and the price of materials in the building trades followed the same fate. Extensive research done by de la Roncière shows that the price of lime dropped by about 20 percent between 1336 and 1340 and stayed at depressed levels in the following years.[41] Wages of masons between 1340 and 1347 averaged 25 to 45 percent lower than wages paid in the preceding decade.[42]

In this scenario, the occurrence of the famine in 1347 deepened the disequilibrium of the market. Operating on the supply side, the crop failure created a severe shortage of foodstuffs, the demand for which was scarcely elastic. Thus, while total effective demand, nonagricultural prices, wages, and rents were all depressed, the prices of foodstuffs increased, with the price of wheat going up by more than 100 percent. This meant a redistribution of income in favor of land-

---

[39]G. Villani, *Cronica* XI, 138.

[40]Sapori, "Pigioni di case e botteghe," pp. 22–23.

[41]Ch. M. de la Roncière, *Florence centre économique regional au XIVe siècle*, vol. 4 (Aix-en-Provence, 1976), p. 495.

[42]De la Roncière, *Florence*, vol. 1, pp. 296 and 343.

owners. It was not only a question of more misery among the poor. Since the marginal propensity to save of the agricultural producers was in all likelihood higher than the propensity to save of the consumers, the ultimate effect of the famine was to further depress the demand for nonagricultural products. At the same time, the export of hard currency to finance grain imports reduced domestic income and deepened the already severe shortage of money and credit. Paradoxically, therefore, though it pushed up some prices the famine added to the severity of the deflation.

III

Through one of those unfortunate and quite unforeseen coincidences that take every rational mind by surprise, between 1345 and 1347, in the very middle of this catastrophic crisis, there suddenly occurred a drastic rise in the price of silver. The origins of this rise were quite exogenous to the Florentine economic system, but had consequences (for reasons we shall go into later) that threatened to further aggravate the serious deflation already prevailing. To understand this other act in our drama we must turn our attention to the market in precious metals.

It is not easy to determine precisely the exchange ratio between gold and silver in medieval times (a ratio henceforth indicated by the symbol AU/AR). There is an apparent abundance of data that have been calculated even to three or four decimal places, but they are largely spurious, for they reflect not only the AU/AR ratio, but also the differential costs of minting, the cost of the copper alloy, and possible premiums in favor of specific coins.[43] Having made these reservations, I must add that if we renounce the claim to an unrealistic precision it is still possible to argue in terms of both orders of magnitude and general trends. And then the following picture emerges.

About the middle of the thirteenth century, the AU/AR ratio in Northern Italy must have stood at between 1:9 and 1:11. In other words, one needed nine to eleven units of silver to obtain one unit of gold. In 1252, Genoa and Florence initiated a regular gold coinage, reintroducing into Christian Europe the bimetallic sys-

[43]A document from Treviso of 1311 records that a gold mark was reckoned at that time to be worth thirteen silver marks, but documents so explicit about the exchange ratio between gold and silver in the Middle Ages are very rare. In order to get an idea of the ratio, historians are usually forced to resort to the exchange rates between gold and silver coins (when such rates are available), but these rates are not a good proxy. Clearly one should use only market rates, and the coins in question must have circulated as full-bodied money. But even when these conditions are satisfied the results may be misleading. The rate of exchange between a gold coin and a silver one can reflect not only the AU/AR ratio, but also a premium favoring one of the two coins considered. Furthermore, there may have been several denominations in circulation, and normally the smaller denominations contained proportionately less pure metal to compensate for the greater cost of minting. For example, as we shall see later, at the beginning of the fourteenth century there were three silver coins in circulation in Florence: the *denaro* at 240 to the *lira*, the *quattrino* at 60 to the *lira*, and the *grosso guelfo* of 30 *denari* at 8 to the *lira*. In theory and practice, therefore, 8 *grossi* equaled 60 *quattrini* or 240 *denari*. But 8 *grossi* contained 15.7 grams of pure silver, 60 *quattrini* contained 13 grams, and 240 *denari* 12.6 grams. (Cf. Appendix, Table D.) If the AU/AR ratio is calculated on the basis of the exchange rate between the gold florin and the silver currency, it is obvious that the results will be quite different, depending on whether one chooses the *grosso*, the *quattrino*, or the *denaro* as the reference coin. Most figures referred to in current literature as measures of the AU/AR ratio are spurious measures that reflect both the ratio in question and other factors.

tem. Venice followed their example in 1284.[44] Partly because of the new and growing demand for gold for monetary use, gold appreciated continuously with respect to silver during the second half of the century. Between 1310 and 1320, the AU/AR ratio in Northern Italy reached and exceeded the level of 1:14.

Then, with the 1340s, the situation was unexpectedly reversed. In January 1343 a substantial influx of gold was reported at the mint in Venice. In May and June of the same year, Venetian documents speak of "very great quantities" of gold brought in by sea.[45] Two years later, in 1345, G. Villani noted that "there was in Florence a great lack of silver currency and no silver coins except the coins of four [that is, the *quattrini*] because all silver coins were melted down and carried overseas." According to Villani, the price of silver had risen to more than 8.28 gold florins for every pound (339.5 grams) of 11.5/12 (958.3/1000) fineness. Two years later still, in August 1347, Villani reported that the silver pound of 958.3/1000 fineness had further risen to 8.79 florins, and that "merchants were rounding it [the silver] up for profit and carrying it overseas where it was much in demand."[46]

[44]The kings of England and France instituted gold coinage in 1257 and 1266 respectively, but on a reduced and irregular scale. France began to mint gold coins effectively only in 1290s, and on a larger scale only with the issue of the *écu à la chaise* in 1337. In England a continuous and regular gold coinage began in 1344.

[45]R. Cessi, *Problemi monetari veneziani* (Padua, 1937), p. 81, doc. 97; p. 82, doc. 99; p. 83, doc. 100.

[46]G. Villani (*Cronica* XII, 53 and 97) quotes for 1345 the price of "more than 12 *lire a fiorino*" and for 1347 the price of 12 *lire* and 15 *soldi a fiorino*. The *lira a fiorino* was a unit of account representing 20/29 of a gold florin. Thus the two prices Villani mentions for 1345 and 1347 meant respectively 8.28 and 8.79 florins.

The Venetian and Florentine accounts confirm and complete each other, and if we accept the prices quoted for silver by Villani (and we have no reason to doubt their validity) we must conclude that in Florence the AU/AR ratio had fallen to 1:11 in 1345 and in August 1347 it had further dropped to 1:10.5.[47] Compared with the ratio prevailing twenty years earlier, silver had thus appreciated in relation to gold by more than 30 percent.

This development has never been adequately explained.[48] In 1347, when Villani wrote of the revaluation of silver in Florence, Ibn Batuta recorded a fall in

[47]The AU/AR ratio is derived from the data supplied by Villani in the following way. According to Villani (see previous footnote), in 1345 one pound of silver of 958.3/1000 fineness was worth more than 8.28 gold florins. By simple proportion it can be calculated that a pound (=339.5 grams) of pure silver (of 1000/1000 fineness) must have been worth about 8.64 gold florins. Estimating the gold florin at 3.53 grams of pure gold, one finds that 339.5 grams of pure silver were the equivalent of more than 30.5 grams of pure gold. Hence an AU/AR ratio of about 1:11.

Similar calculations can be carried out for 1347. If one pound of silver of 958.3/1000 fineness was worth 8.79 florins, one pound of pure silver (1000/1000) must have been worth 9.17 gold florins, or 32.4 grams of pure gold. Hence an AU/AR ratio of about 1:10.5.

[48]B. Homan "La circolazione delle monete d'oro in Ungheria dal X al XIV secolo e la crisi europea dell'oro nel secolo XIV," in *Rivista italiana di numismatica* [1922], wrote that "the crisis of silver in 1344 and 1345 . . . was certainly caused by the Queen of Hungary's journey to Italy in 1343–1344." Hungary was a large producer of gold at that time, and Homan, relying on the chronicle of John, Archdeacon of Kukullo, maintains that the widow of Carlo Roberto went to Naples in 1343–1344 to help her son, heir apparent to the throne, taking with her 27,000 marks of pure silver, 17,000 marks of pure gold, and some gold florins. Because these amounts were not enough, she received a further sum of 4,000 marks of gold from her son, Ludwig the Great. According to Homan, this influx of gold caused the value of gold to fall.

I do not know how reliable the figures reported by the Archdeacon of Kukullo are, but the explanation offered by Homan seems

the value of gold in relation to silver in the Middle East.[49] In Egypt, the AU/AR ratio fell from about 1:12 in 1339 to little more than 1:7 about 1348.[50] In China, the official ratio dropped from about 1:10 in 1309 to about 1:4 in 1375.[51] Whether the origin of the upheaval was in

naive to say the least. Among other things it takes no account of the fact that Venetian sources state explicitly that the gold entering Venice "in great quantity" came there "by sea" (Cessi, *Problemi monetari* pp. 82 and 83) and that G. Villani, mentioning the rise in the price of silver in 1345, states that silver collected from the melting of coins "was carried overseas" (G. Villani, *Cronica* XII, 53). I think that the journey of Carlo Roberto's widow and the figures of the Archdeacon of Kukullo can be quietly shelved, and that one should instead focus attention on overseas markets. R. H. Bautier ("L'or et l'argent en Occident de la fin du *XIIIe* siècle au debut du *XIVe* siècle," *Comptes-rendus* of the Académie des inscriptions et belles lettres de Paris [1951], p. 173), after asserting that "the essential cause" of the revaluation of silver was "incontestably" the outbreak of the Hundred Years' War between France and England, states that the rise in the value of silver in the period 1340–1349 was due to the interruption of commerce between the West and the Mongols, and to the reopening of trade with Egypt, an event that would have caused a substantial outflow of silver from Europe. Apart from the internal contradictions of Bautier's double "explanation," its shakiness lies in its completely hypothetical nature; it is based on three assumptions, viz. that (a) there occurred a dramatic reorientation of commercial flows; (b) there was no deficit in Europe's balance of trade with the Mongols or, if there was one, it was not settled with silver; (c) there was a deficit in Europe's balance of trade with Egypt and this deficit was settled by the exports of silver. None of these assumptions can be documented.

[49]Ibn Batuta, *The Travels*, H. A. R. Gibb, trans. (Cambridge, England, 1958–1962), part 1, pp. 247–248.

[50]A. M. Watson, "Back to Gold and Silver," *The Economic History Review*, ser. 2, vol. 20 (1967), p. 27, tab. 2; E. Ashtor, *Les métaux précieux et la balance des payements du proche Orient à la basse époque* (Paris, 1971), p. 48.

[51]Leng-Scheng Yang, *Money and Credit in China* Cambridge, Mass., 1952), p. 48; E. Biot, "Mémoire sur le systéme monétaire des Chinois," *Journal Asiatique*, ser. 3, vol. 4 (1837), pp. 445 and 452; Hsin-wei Peng, *Chung-kuo huo-pi* (Peking, 1954), pp. 414–416 and 456; Chien-hung Li, *Sung Yüan Ming Ching-chi shih-lun* (Peking, 1957), pp. 97–100.

the Far East or the Middle East is not important here. What is clear is that somewhere in the East some significant event took place which led to a drastic revaluation of silver with respect to gold. The AU/AR ratio reached lower levels in the Orient than in Europe, where gold had been continuously revaluing for more than half a century. Consequently there was a massive exportation of silver from Europe to the East and an influx of gold from the East into Europe.

In order to assess the impact of these events on the economic situation in Florence, it is necessary to explain certain basic aspects of the Florentine monetary system of the period.

IV

On the eve of the great crash, say, in 1338, the monetary system of Florence consisted of the following coins: the gold florin, the silver *grosso* (groat), the *quattrino*, and the *denaro picciolo*. These coins stood in the following relationships:

1 florin	=	±744 *denari*
1 *grosso*	=	30 *denari*
1 *quattrino*	=	4 *denari*

Attention must be drawn to the ± sign that qualifies the equivalence between the florin and the *denaro*. Let us look at the reasons for this sign and the complications it involves.

The monetary authorities never succeeded in stabilizing the exchange rate between the gold florin and the *denaro*. In the short run it was impossible to maintain a stable rate of exchange between gold and silver coins when the market exchange ratio between the two metals was characteristically unstable. In the long run, the source of instability that proved to be by far the most important was the progressive debasement of the *denaro*. With the minting first of the silver *grosso* and then of a gold coin the Italian states had intended to create fixed multiples of the *denaro* and at the same time provide international trade and finance with means of payment that were stable in their metallic content. The two purposes however, proved to be incompatible. The intrinsic stability of the gold currency—the means of payment *par excellence* in international financial transactions and trade—was never in doubt. Consequently all inflationary pressures fell upon the lesser currency. Thus while the gold coin remained intrinsically stable, the *denaro* was progressively debased. As a result, the gold florin and the silver *denaro* did not become integral parts of a single monetary system, but represented the basic elements of two parallel systems,[52] one jealously protected from inflationary pressures, the other fully exposed to them.

In the dual monetary system just described, the silver *grosso* was in an ambiguous position, for it was

[52]The failure to integrate the florin and the *denaro* into a single monetary system made it necessary to keep alive two parallel systems of abstract units of account, representing respectively the abstract submultiples of the gold coin and the abstract multiples of the *denaro*. In Florence the two systems were as follows (the units of account are indicated by italics):

I: 1 gold florin = 29 *soldi a fiorino*
   1 *lira a fiorino* = 20 *soldi a fiorino*
                    = 240 *denari a fiorino*

II: 1 *lira di denari piccioli* = 20 *soldi di denari*
                              = 60 quattrini
                              = 240 denari

unclear whether it should be part of the hard system or the soft one. By definition the *grosso* was *moneta grossa* and thus should have belonged to the stable system of the gold currency. In practice, however, things worked out differently, and in this respect it is interesting to note the different behavior of the monetary authorities in Venice and Florence. Because the Venetian *grosso* had acquired a position of prestige in Oriental trade that the Florentine *grosso* never enjoyed in international dealings, Venice made every effort to preserve the stability of its *grosso*, whereas Florence allowed its *grosso* to follow the fate of the *denaro*, although resorting to ingenious maneuvers designed to mask its actual debasement.[53]

The existence of two parallel monetary systems gave rise to two parallel systems of prices. Inevitably, the system of domestic prices remained tied to the system of the *denaro*. Two factors fundamentally prevented the internal price system from being based on gold, namely: (1) the gold coin had too high a unitary value to serve as the measure of value and medium of exchange in many of the current domestic transactions; (2) if the system of domestic prices had been allowed to rest on gold, all the inflationary pressures that were acting on the small currency would have been laid on the gold coinage.[54]

[53]In contrast to the *grosso*, the *quattrino* in Florence and the *soldino* in Venice never found themselves in the ambiguous position of the *grosso*. For all practical purposes, the *quattrino* was always considered petty currency and therefore followed the fortunes of the *denaro*, eventually taking the *denaro's* place when this coin became so small and lightweight as to be unusable.

[54]In 1294 the Commune of Florence prohibited the fixing of wages for the Commune's employees in gold and ordered that they be fixed in petty currency. The ordinance was reconfirmed in 1316 (M. Ber-

The two monetary flows (that of the gold florin and that of the silver currency) remained largely though not completely separate. Members of the lower classes not infrequently had florins in their hands,[55] but the two flows tended to be identified with different sections of society, as well as with different economic areas. Given these circumstances, the fact that the rate of exchange between the florin and the *denaro* (or the *quattrino*, for that matter) was a floating rate and not a fixed one had both social and economic implications.

Fundamentally, a rise in the quotation of the florin in terms of petty coinage tended to have an expansionary and inflationary effect on the economy, whereas a fall tended to have a depressive and deflationary effect. The exporters and producers favored and were favored by a rise in the exchange rate. G. Villani wrote that "the clothiers pay their workers in small coins and sell their cloth for florins" and therefore a weak florin caused them "great distress."[56] Marchionne di Coppo Stefani echoed this: "the lesser artisans are paid in *soldi*; the merchants sell for florins and pay the work done for them in *soldi*; thus the merchants pressed for a

nocchi, *Il sistema monetario fiorentino e le leggi del governo popolare del 1378–1382* [Bologna, 1979], p. 15). At the beginning of the fourteenth century it was also decreed that only Calimala merchants, money changers, cloth and silk manufacturers, and furriers could fix their prices and keep their accounts in florins; all other businesses had to make use of the petty currency (R. de Roover, *The Rise and Decline of the Medici Bank 1397–1494* [New York, 1966], p. 32). Restraints of this kind were inspired by the same logic by which the linking of obligations to the price of gold is normally prohibited today. But in Florence it was not illegal to contract loans in gold currency (de la Roncière, *Florence*, vol. 2, p. 530).

[55] R. A. Goldthwaite, *The Building of Renaissance Florence* (Baltimore and London, 1980), pp. 304–305.

[56] G. Villani, *Cronica* XII, 97 and 53.

strong florin, especially the clothiers and those who lived on rents."[57] The argument requires elaboration. In a city-state like Florence a large part of the commerce was international, and much of the production was for export. As already stated, gold coins were the typical means of payment in international trade, whereas domestic prices and wages were generally reckoned in the unit of account based on the petty currency. In this situation, if wages did not increase simultaneously and proportionately with the exchange rate, every rise in the quotation of the florin meant a reduction of the cost of labor in terms of the florin itself.[58] On the other hand, insofar as the level of domestic prices did not immediately and proportionately adjust to the rise in the exchange rate and insofar as the external demand was price-elastic, the rise in the rate of the florin stimulated exports because commodities became less expensive in terms of gold, which was the currency with which the foreign importer made his payments. Therefore, when the florin was on the rise, the Florentine businessman could either keep the price of his own merchandise unchanged in terms of florins and profit from the reduction in costs as expressed in that currency, or he could lower the price of his goods for export in terms of florins and profit from the increased volume of business; or else he could choose the best

[57]Marchionne di Coppo Stefani, "Cronaca Fiorentina," *Rerum italicarum scriptores*, vol. 30, part 1 (Cittá di Castello, 1903), rubr. 877.

[58]Goldthwaite, *The Building of Renaissance Florence*, pp. 304–305, points out that in a number of cases wages were paid in gold pieces. However, this does not contradict the argument set forth in the text. What matters is that wages were *reckoned* in petty currency. Thus if the rate of change increased, a given wage was paid in a smaller number of gold pieces.

combination of these alternatives. All this is in the case of a lag of wages and internal prices in relation to a rise in the quotation of the florin. In the case of a lead, the rise of the quotation served to keep the Florentine exporters competitive on the international market. Because of mechanisms exactly opposite those just described, a fall in the florin meant loss of competitiveness for the Florentine exporters.

Actually, merchant bankers and clothiers were not the only class of people who gained by the strengthening of the florin and lost by its fall. In the passage quoted earlier, Marchionne di Coppo Stefani mentioned also "those who lived on rents." If the rent was reckoned in florins, the landlord profited. But many rents were reckoned in the money of account based on the silver currency. I think that in the phrase "those who lived on rent" Marchionne was referring to the large landowners who sold the products of the soil wholesale, and therefore in florins, and paid their workers in petty coinage.

De la Roncière has shown that the majority of loans, even those for small amounts, were reckoned in florins.[59] This obviously reflected the greater bargaining power of the lenders over the borrowers. At any rate, the coexistence of the two monetary systems produced a situation in which the creditors benefited from the depreciation of the petty currency. Doctors and lawyers also received the greater part of their fees in florins, so we may assume they too would be aligned with the bankers and clothiers.

To conclude, among those who gained from a strengthening of the florin and conversely suffered

[59]De la Roncière, *Florence*, vol. 2, p. 530.

from its weakness were not only the clothiers, but also the bankers, the merchant houses, the moneylenders, the doctors, the lawyers, and the big landed proprietors. These were in essence the members of the patriciate and of the so-called *Arti Maggiori* (the greater Guilds).[60]

The movements in the rate of the florin essentially produced a redistribution of income. Thus if some individuals profited from a rise of the rate others lost by it. These others were the shopkeepers and the craftsmen, most of whom belonged to the *Arti Minori* (the lesser Guilds),[61] the wage earners who had no guilds of their own, and the state employees.

The shopkeepers were hurt by the rise of the florin because they bought in florins and sold in silver currency. As to craftsmen and wage earners, their compensations were reckoned in the money of account based on the petty currency. Insofar as they acquired goods and services priced in petty currency, the rise of the quotation of the florin should have left them indifferent. But also among the wage earners and especially among the craftsmen were individuals who strove to put away a few florins as a stable store of value or dreamed about buying a small house or a little piece of land that they would have to pay for in florins.[62]

[60]The seven greater guilds were those of judges and notaries, merchants of Calimala, bankers and money changers, doctors and apothecaries, wool manufacturers, silk manufacturers, and skinners and furriers.

[61]The *Arti Minori* were those of the butchers, shoemakers, blacksmiths, master stone masons and wood-carvers, retail dealers and linen merchants, wine merchants, bakers, oil merchants, locksmiths, tanners, armorers, innkeepers, saddlers, and carpenters.

[62]See what was already said in footnote 58 regarding Goldthwaite's observation (in *The Building of Renaissance Florence*, pp. 304–

It should also be made clear that people were aware of a positive, if rough, correlation between the movements of the florin and the movements of the general level of prices expressed in petty currency. In fact, they tended to see in the rate of the florin the index of the worth of local currency and hence of the cost of living. When relating the price of victuals, contemporary chroniclers generally also quoted the current rate of the florin: clearly in their minds the two things were related. In major cities such as Florence and Siena, an official market rate for the florin was publicized daily[63] and as the bells of the churches reminded people of the passing of time and of their duties, so the daily quotation of the florin made everybody in town acutely aware of the health of their local currency.

The coexistence in the same market of two currencies, one strong and one weak, was bound to exacerbate the frustration and the protest of those whose incomes were pegged to the weak currency when this currency gave signs of further weakening. In Bologna in 1352, when the florin rose to 34 *soldi* the employees of the Commune refused to accept petty coins in payment for their wages. A group of workers took a similar stand in Bergamo in 1371, when the quotation of

305) that workers were occasionally paid in florins. In a discussion about the rise of the gold ducat in Genoa in 1488 it was stated that the rise "should be of concern to everybody but especially to the workers who receive the same wage that they received when the ducat was of lower value" ("ad omnes pertinet maxime etiam ad pauperes qui suam mercedem talem accipiunt qualem acciperunt in minori precio ducati") (Archivio di Stato, Genoa, Membranacei di San Giorgio, LXXXV, Constitutiones et ordinationes Domus Ceche, meeting of October 21, 1488).

[63]For Florence see M. Bernocchi, *Le monete della repubblica fiorentina*, vol. 4 (Florence, 1974–1978), pp. v–xx.

the florin was rising: as a document of the time puts it, a local entrepreneur "wanted to give them [the workers] petty coins and the workers did not want them."[64]

In sum, the question of the relative value of the gold florin and the local silver currency was not one of interest only to the bankers and a few big merchants. It was, on the contrary, a question of preeminent general interest with all the potential of causing widespread social tension and unrest. One must keep these considerations in mind if one wants to understand the logic of the monetary policies and developments of fourteenth-century Florence.

The crisis that struck the financial oligarchy in the 1340s opened a new chapter in the political history of Florence: in 1343 a new regime was installed that was decidedly more "democratic" than its predecessors.[65] The mass of the wage earners—those who could be described anachronistically as the proletariat—and some other groups remained without representation. But the lower and middle elements of the guild community (craftsmen, shopkeepers, dyers, and furriers, that is, in essence, the members of the *Arti Minori*) obtained seats in the administration. The plague of 1348, making labor both scarce and expensive, further

[64]C. M. Cipolla, *Studi di storia della moneta: i movimenti dei cambi in Italia dal secolo XIII al secolo XV* (Pavia, 1948), p. 123, n. 2.

[65]Among the more recent works on Florentine government and politics for the period 1343–1378, see Brucker, *Florentine Politics,* and M. Becker, *Florence in Transition* (Baltimore, 1967–1969). Among the classics see G. Salvemini, *Magnati e Popolani in Firenze dal 1280 al 1295* (Florence, 1899); N. Rodolico, *La democrazia fiorentina nel suo tramonto* (Bologna, 1905); N. Rodolico, *I Ciompi: una pagina di storia del proletariato operaio* (Florence, 1945).

strengthened the power of this group. Weak in the first five years of the new regime, the position of the *Arti Minori* strengthened after 1348 and especially after October 1350, when the *Arti Minori* succeeded in restoring their number of representatives from seven to the original fourteen.

After 1350, "the political forces within the regime were so nicely balanced that no single group predominated, although there were temporary upheavals and dislocations. Practicing caution and restraint, politicians tended to avoid precipitate action which might recoil against them or which could destroy the uneasy balance."[66] The policy that then prevailed, as Professor Brucker puts it, was one of compromise. This policy is most visible at the monetary level, where a compromise clearly prevailed between those who had everything to gain from the rise of the florin (patricians and members of the *Arti Maggiori*) and those who on the contrary were acutely interested in the strength of the petty currency (craftsmen and shopkeepers of the *Arti Minori*). The outcome of the compromise was a policy of monetary stability.

[66]Brucker, *Florentine Politics* p. 148. See also pp. 387ff.

CHAPTER II

The Devaluations of 1345 and 1347

I

AT THIS point, the reader should be in a position to understand what the rise in the price of silver in the years 1345–1347 meant to the Florentine economy. The great economic expansion between the mid-thirteenth century and the beginning of the fourteenth had been favored by, among other factors, the rising quotation of the gold florin, which in 1252 was worth 240 *denari* and by the beginning of the fourteenth century had risen to about 780. The rise in the value of silver in the 1340s reversed the trend, and it could not have occurred at a worse moment. It was a depressive and deflationary factor,[1] which happened to appear in the very middle of a deflationary crisis, adding to its already exceptional severity. Furthermore, it represented an element of potential conflict in a delicate social and political

[1]The effect was deflationary in the sense that the revaluation of silver tended to depress prices expressed in petty currency. As previously indicated, the system of domestic prices was based on that currency.

equilibrium that had only just been formed with the entry of the *Arti Minori* into the active political arena in 1343. Let us trace the chain of events that followed at the monetary level.

Before 1345, the silver coins in circulation in Florence had the following content of pure silver (1000/1000):

> 1 *denaro* contained 0.0524 grams
> 1 *quattrino* (4 *denari*) contained 0.217 grams
> 1 *grosso* (30 *denari*) contained 1.96 grams

The silver content of the coins was not proportionate to their face value. This is easily seen by calculating the silver equivalent of a *lira* when paid in the different kinds of coins (see Appendix, Table D). The *lira*, the unit of account based on the silver currency, was equal by definition to 240 *denari*, 60 (240/4) *quattrini*, or 8 (240/30) *grossi*. Turning these values into grams of pure silver, one finds that one *lira* was equal to:

> 12.58 grams if paid in (240) *denari*;
> 13.02 grams if paid in (60) *quattrini*;
> 15.68 grams if paid in (8) *grossi*.

Therefore between the silver equivalent of the *lira* when paid in *grossi* and the silver equivalent when paid in *denari* there was a difference of about 25 percent— quite a sizable difference, but not difficult to account for. The production of smaller coins entailed higher labor costs, because from the same weight of metal a greater number of pieces had to be obtained. Furthermore, in the lower denominations a larger quantity of copper was mixed with the silver. To compensate for these higher costs of production, the amount of silver in the smaller coins was reduced proportionately.

We now come to 1345. The pressure of the rise of

silver had been felt for some time, as evidenced both by Venetian documents discussed above in Chapter I and by the behavior of the florin on various markets.[2] With 1345, the situation became painfully acute. In Florence the price of a pound (339.5 grams) of silver of 958.3/1000 fineness reached the price of about 8.28 gold florins.[3] At the current rate of about 62 *soldi* (i.e., 744 *denari*) to the florin, 8.28 florins equaled about 6,160 *denari*. At that price it was no longer worthwhile for anybody to take silver to the mint to have it transformed into coins, because the face value of the currency to be obtained was below the market value of the metal. In fact, a pound of silver of 958.3/1000 fineness would have yielded currency in the amount of only 4,890 to 5,216 *denari* when made into *grossi*; made into *quattrini* it would have yielded the equivalent of about 5,656 *denari*.[4] Another way of saying the same thing (but ignoring the costs of minting) is to state that at the price reached by the metal on the bullion market the

[2] On the quotation of the florin on the various Italian markets, see C. M. Cipolla, *Studi di storia della moneta: i movimenti dei cambi in Italia dal secolo XII al secolo XV* (Pavia, 1948).

[3] See above, Chapt. 1, footnote 46.

[4] Anyone bringing a pound of silver of 958.3/1000 fineness to the mint and requesting *grossi* would have received 163 pieces (the mint striking 166 coins and retaining 3 for rights of seigniorage). The current value of the *grosso* was then 30 to 32 *denari* (see following note), thus 163 *grossi* had a face value of 4,890 to 5,216 *denari*. Whoever took silver to the mint to obtain *grossi* would therefore incur a loss of 15– 30 percent. Anyone bringing a pound of silver of 958.3/1000 fineness to the mint and requesting *quattrini* would have obtained 1,414 pieces (the mint returned 246 *quattrini* on a pound of 166.7/1000 fineness, striking 261 and keeping 15 for seigniorial rights). The *quattrini* had a current face value of 4 *denari*; hence 1,414 *quattrini* had a face value of 5,656 *denari*. Therefore whoever took silver to the mint to obtain *quattrini* would incur a loss of 8.2 percent.

value of the silver contained in the *grossi* and *quattrini* was greater than their face value, namely,[5]

Coin	Face value (in *denari*)	Value of silver content (in *denari*)
grosso	30–32	37.20
quattrino	4	4.10
denaro	1	.99

In these circumstances, not only was it unprofitable to take silver to the mint, it was worthwhile to round up silver coins on the market, melt them down, and sell the metal. Anyone who collected *grossi* on the market and melted them would theoretically make a gross profit (disregarding the costs of melting) on the order of 16–24 percent. Anyone doing the same thing with

[5]The table is based on the following:

Grosso. Face value=30 *denari.* According to Pegolotti, *La pratica della mercatura,* p. 192, however, the *grosso* was also exchanged for 32 *denari.* As to the value of the silver content, the *grossi* current before the reform of 1345 were of 958.3/1000 fineness, and were issued at the rate of 166 pieces per pound (of 339.5 grams). Each *grosso* therefore contained 2.05 grams of silver of 958.3/1000 fineness, which at the current price of about 6,160 *denari* per pound were worth about 37.20 *denari.*

Quattrino. The *quattrini* were issued at the rate of 261 pieces per pound of 166.7/1000 fineness. A *quattrino* contained therefore about 0.226 grams of silver of 958.3/1000 fineness, which at the price of 6,160 *denari* per pound were worth about 4.10 *denari.*

Denaro. The *denari* then current were issued at the rate of 540 pieces per pound of 83.3/1000 fineness. One *denaro* therefore contained about 0.0546 grams of silver of 958.3/1000 fineness, which at the price of 6,160 *denari* per pound were worth about 0.99 *denari.*

The silver content in the various coins as calculated in this note differs from that calculated in the Appendix, Table D because here we refer to silver of 958.3/1000 fineness, while in the Appendix the calculation is made with reference to pure silver (1000/1000).

the *quattrini* would theoretically make a profit of roughly 2.5 percent.[6] There was nothing to be gained by melting the *denari*.

I said "theoretical" profits because the calculations refer to the theoretical metallic content of the coins in question. In practice, the coins, and especially the smallest ones—*quattrini* and *denari*—were subject to a high rate of wear, and most of the pieces in circulation weighed less than what they were theoretically supposed to. It follows that those who melted down petty coins extracted less silver than indicated in the preceding calculations. Speculation must therefore have concentrated on the *grosso*, and indeed G. Villani confirmed this when he wrote that only the *quattrino* among the silver currency remained in circulation.[7]

A difficult situation then developed. Nobody brought silver to the mint to obtain coins. On the other hand speculators rounded up groats on the market to melt them down and export the metal. And all this happened in the middle of a crisis in which (as we have seen in the preceding chapter) credit was shrinking, the velocity of circulation of money was diminishing, and, as the chronicler testified, "ready money was lacking and hardly to be found."[8] Mint documents of August 1345 mention "many complaints made by many manufacturers and other honorable citizens" that

[6]The gross profit in this case is given by the difference between the value of the metallic content and the face value of the coin. The calculation ignores not only the expense of melting, but also the value of the copper that could eventually be recovered.

[7]G. Villani, *Cronica* XII, 53. The *denaro picciolo* also remained in circulation, but Villani correctly considered that not as silver currency but as billon.

[8]G. Villani, *Cronica* XI, 138.

"at present no silver money is minted nor is it in use." The authorities admitted that the lack of silver currency caused "the citizens of said city [Florence] many inconveniences and wants."[9] If the authorities in charge of monetary affairs showed themselves particularly concerned with the "inconveniences and wants" of the citizenry, G. Villani warns us that their preoccupation also had other motives. The increase in the value of silver and the diminution of the quantity of silver currency in circulation was forcing down the quotation of the florin, and for the reasons illustrated in the preceding chapter a weakening of the florin hurt the entrepreneurial classes: "Wherefore there is great distress to the clothiers and other manufacturers, they being afraid lest the florin fall too much."[10]

The only possible solution to these problems was the devaluation of the silver currency. However, at this point a serious problem arose. The silver currency that was the target of the speculation was not the *denaro* or even the *quattrino* but the *grosso,* and the debasement of the *grosso* was not a measure that the authorities would undertake lightly.

In Venice, where an analogous situation had arisen, the problem was even more difficult than in Florence. The Venetian *grosso* was a popular means of exchange in the Levantine trade, and one of the reasons for its vast popularity was the coin's time-honored metallic stability. For Venice to debase the *grosso* meant risking the prestige of a currency that had served her nobly in

[9]M. Bernocchi, *Le monete della repubblica fiorentina* (Florence, 1974–1978), vol. 1, pp. 82 and 87.

[10]G. Villani, *Cronica* XII, 53.

penetrating the Middle Eastern markets. The rather crude solution devised by the Venetian authorities clearly shows the difficult situation in which they were floundering. They left the *grosso* untouched but instead depreciated the half *grosso* (called *mezzanino*), reducing its intrinsic content from 0.97 to 0.78 grams of pure silver.[11] The consequences were such as might be expected. The minting of *grossi* practically ceased, and the *grossi* already in circulation were either melted down or circulated at a premium.[12]

In Florence, the most important currency in large-scale trade and international finance was by far the gold florin. Yet even in Florence there was strong resistance to debasing the *grosso* which—like all *"moneta grossa"*—was commonly accepted outside the territory of Florence and served widely as a means of payment in most parts of central Italy. To debase the *grosso* would have meant putting this coin on the same level as the petty currency, which because of its instability had a more local, restricted circulation.

Faced with this dilemma the Florentines acted with remarkable skill, proving themselves fully aware of the importance of psychological factors in financial affairs. A new *grosso* was minted of considerably higher face value than that of the preceding *grosso*: that is, whereas the old *grosso* was worth 30 *denari* (2–1/2 *soldi*), the newly minted *grosso* was issued at the nominal face value of 48 *denari* (4 *soldi*). However, the silver content of the new coin was not increased proportion-

---

[11]N. Papadopoli, *Le monete di Venezia* (Venice, 1893–1907), vol. 1, p. 174.

[12]*Ibid.*, pp. 173–175.

ately. The old *grosso* contained 1.96 grams of pure silver, and the new one, 2.46 grams.[13] In other words, whereas the face value was increased by 60 percent, the silver content was increased by only 25 percent. In form the *grosso* came from the mint larger and heavier than before. In substance, a depreciation of about 20 percent had taken place (see Appendix, Table D). It was a conjuring trick—but it worked. Giovanni Villani commented: "And it was a very handsome coin . . . and had a large circulation in Florence and throughout Tuscany."[14] And Marchionne di Coppo Stefani echoed: "it was a good and handsome coin."[15]

The nominal value of the new *grosso* was greater than its intrinsic value by about 11 percent: the nominal value being 4 *soldi*, namely 48 *denari*, whereas the

[13]The mint ordinance of August 19, 1345, directed that the new *grosso* be issued at the rate of 134 pieces to the pound, which meant a theoretical weight of 2.53 grams apiece. But four days later the ordinance was amended to the effect that the new *grosso* be struck at the rate of 132 pieces to the pound, which meant a theoretical weight of 2.57 grams. The fineness being 958.3/1000, the amount of pure silver (1000/1000) in the coin was theoretically 2.46 grams. (Bernocchi, *Le monete*, vol. 1, pp. 81ff and 86ff; vol. 3, pp. 179–181).

On the basis of a passage in G. Villani, *Cronica* XII, 53, Bernocchi postulates that in October 1345 a second amendment ordered the coining to be at 142 *grossi* to the pound (*Le monete*, vol. 1, pp. 180–181). But Ch. M. de la Roncière, *Florence centre économique regionale au XIVe siècle*, vol. 4 (Aix-en-Provence, 1976), p. 111, n. 63, has convincingly demonstrated that Villani was inexact. The amendment of August 23 was simply put into effect in October without any additional variations. (Incidentally the documents quoted by de la Roncière were known also to Bernocchi; see *Le monete*, vol. 1, p. xxxix.)

[14]G. Villani, *Cronica* XII, 53.

[15]Marchionne di Coppo Stefani, "Cronica fiorentina," *Rerum italicarum scriptores*, vol. 30, part 1 (Cittá di Castello, 1903), rubr. 624.

value of the silver content was 43.6 *denari*.[16] It was therefore profitable to take metal to the mint to obtain new
grossi. Between the 12th and the 31st of October 1345,[17]
116,138 new *grossi* were coined,[18] worth 23,228 *lire* (we
do not know how much of this minting originated from
melting down old *grossi*). In the following half year,
from November 1345 to April 1346, more *grossi* were
coined,[19] but we do not know the amount of the issue.[20]
On the other hand, there were no requests for either
quattrini or *denari* because it was to nobody's advantage
to have them coined. The ordinances of August 1345
had ignored these two small coins. The reason we already know: speculation had focused on the *grosso*, and
the monetary authorities had moved to block the effects
of that speculation. The authorities must also have considered the amount of *quattrini* and *denari* in circulation
to be adequate to the needs of trade, and that it would
be better to avoid the inflationary pressures that might
result from a combined depreciation of the petty currency. But devaluing the *grosso* yet keeping the old *quat-*

[16]The calculation is based on the following data: the *grosso* of 4
soldi of 1345 was of 958.3/1000 fineness and was struck at the rate of
132 pieces per pound (339.5 grams). Each *grosso* therefore contained
2.57 grams of silver at 958.3/1000 fineness: at the price of about 6,160
denari to the pound (see above, p. 33), the 2.57 grams were worth
43.63 *denari*.

[17]According to the explicit testimony of G. Villani, *Cronica* XII, 53,
the new *grosso* of 4 *soldi* "was issued from the mint for the first time
on the twelfth day of October of that year 1345." This information is
confirmed by contemporary documents. See Bernocchi, *Le monete*,
vol. 1, p. xxxix, and de la Roncière, *Florence*, vol. 4, p. 111, n. 63.

[18]Bernocchi, *Le monete*, vol. 3, p. 252.

[19]*Ibid.*, vol. 1, p. 91.

[20]*Ibid.*, vol. 3, p. 252.

trini and *denari* in circulation meant breaking the alignment between the different denominations. The consequences became evident in 1347.

II

By the summer of 1347, according to Giovanni Villani, the price of a pound of silver of 958.3/1000 fineness rose still higher, reaching the level of 8.79 gold florins,[21] with an increase of 6.25 percent over the price of two years earlier. The florin was now at 61–62 *soldi* (732–744 *denari*), and at this rate 8.79 florins amounted to about 6,487 *denari*. At this price, the value of the metallic content in the silver coins was once again greater than their face value, as the following data show:[22]

Coin	Face value (in *denari*)	Value of silver content (in *denari*)
grosso of 1345	48	49.11
quattrino	4	4.32
denaro	1	1.04

[21]See above, Chapt. 1, footnote 46.

[22]The value of the silver content of the different coins mentioned in the text is calculated on the basis of the following:

grosso: of 958.3/1000 fineness and issued at the rate of 132 coins per pound of 339.5 grams. Each *grosso* contained therefore 2.57 grams of silver at 958.3/1000 that, at the price of 6,487 *denari* per pound, were worth about 49.11 *denari*.

quattrino: issued at the rate of 261 pieces per pound of silver of 166.7/1000 fineness. A *quattrino* therefore contained about 0.226 grams of silver of 958.3/1000 fineness that, at the price of 6,487 *denari* per pound, were worth about 4.32 *denari*.

denaro: issued at the rate of 540 pieces per pound of silver of 83.3/1000 fineness. A *denaro* therefore contained about 0.0546 grams of silver of 958.3/1000 fineness that, at the price of 6,487 per pound, were worth about 1.04 *denari*.

In these circumstances, anyone who melted down *quattrini* and sold the silver would make a theoretical gross profit of about 8 percent (disregarding the costs of melting, and not counting the value of the copper retrieved in the process); anyone who carried out the same operation with the *denari* would make a theoretical gross profit on the order of 4 percent; whereas anyone melting down *grossi* of 1345 would gain about 2.3 percent. It was the same story as that of two years earlier, but this time the *quattrino* was the most profitable coin to melt.

Villani relates that the silver coins "were melted down and exported" and adds that consequently "the gold florin fell each day and was on the verge of falling below three liras."[23] He may well have been exaggerating,[24] but there can be hardly any doubt that the florin was under a strong downward pressure. The poor outlook for the florin worried the entrepreneurial circles, which allegedly lobbied for a devaluation of the silver currency.[25] On the other hand the authorities could not remain idle in the face of the demonetization of the petty currency by private speculators, just as two years earlier they could not remain idle in the face of

[23]G. Villani, *Cronica* XII, 57.

[24]The data collected by de la Roncière (*Florence*, vol. 4, p. 525) show that in most transactions the florin was still valued at 61–62 *soldi* and was in only few cases traded at 60 *soldi* (that is, three *lire*). Actually if the rate had fallen to below 60 *soldi*, the operation of melting would not have been so profitable.

[25]G. Villani (*Cronica* XII, 57) relates that "the wool clothiers who were interested [in a strong florin] because they paid for work done for them in [denari] *piccioli* and sold their cloth for florins, being powerful in the Commune, caused the said Commune to order new silver currency and new *quattrini*, debasing both."

the demonetization of the *grosso*. Thus in July 1347 the decision was reached to devalue again.

To protect the *quattrino*, the monetary authorities reduced its content by 18 percent from 0.217 grams of pure silver to 0.178 grams.[26] For the *grosso* they repeated the operation of 1345, though on a more limited scale. A new *grosso* was issued with the face value of 5 *soldi*, which meant a 25 percent increase over the face value (4 *soldi*) of the preceding *grosso*. The metallic content was increased, but whereas the 1345 *grosso* contained 2.46 grams of pure silver, the *grosso* of 1347 had a content of 2.78 grams with an increase of only 13 percent. Thus a *grosso* of higher value and greater weight was put in circulation and appearances were saved, but in fact the *grosso* was devalued by about 10 percent (see Appendix, Table D). The differential debasement of the *quattrino* (18 percent) and the *grosso* (about 10 percent) brought a healthy correction to the disequilibrium created in the alignment between the two currencies in 1345, when the *grosso* was debased but the *quattrino* remained unchanged. Nobody bothered about the *denaro picciolo*, which in all likelihood was thought to be on its way to extinction.

The devaluation of 1347 also had a fiscal aspect, which historians have overlooked. To understand this other aspect of our story, we must clarify the institutional arrangement of minting in medieval Florence.

The Commune of Florence did not coin money on its own account. The mint was a communal institution strictly controlled by the Commune, but it operated

[26]Initially (July 19), the authorities considered reducing the metallic content to 0.173 grams, but a few days later (July 28) the original decision was changed, and it was decreed that the *quattrino* should contain 0.178 grams of pure silver (see Appendix, Table D).

only for third parties. In other words, the mint produced money for and on account of those private individuals who brought metal to it. For this service the mint charged a seigniorage, calculated in such a way as to cover the cost of production and in addition provide a profit that the mint passed on to the Commune's treasury. The mint was bound to issue only the types of currency decreed by the communal authorities and to follow their ordinances strictly as to weight, fineness, and design. But the volume of the issues was left to the wish of those private individuals who brought metal to the mint and asked for the kind and amount of currency they wanted.

In a situation like this, the state did not profit directly from a debasement of currency, that is, from a reduction in the metallic content of the coins. Those who profited were the individuals in a position to take metal to the mint when the debasement had been decreed. The state profited only indirectly through the seigniorage tax, the total amount of which was of course proportionate to the volume of the mint's activity.

Having clarified this point, let us now look at what happened in 1347. The communal finances were in desperate straits. We saw in Chapter I that in February 1345 the Commune had had to declare the temporary suspension of payments on its debts. Then came the famine of 1347. The Commune, already bankrupt, overburdened with debts, and having difficulties in paying its employees, found itself having to face great, new, and undeferrable expenditures in order to relieve the hunger, not only of its citizens, but also of the starving people who were flocking in from the countryside. To buy grain, the Commune had to resort to new loans: one of 15,000 florins, then a second one of nearly

6,000 florins; then a third one of 20,000 florins.[27] But loans were not enough. New taxes were resorted to, like that imposed on moneylenders, which brought in some 3,000 florins.[28] Then, in the summer of 1347, in a desperate search for "ways and means to increase the revenues of the Commune," the authorities moved to raise the seigniorage charged by the mint.

It was not by accident that the beleaguered authorities did what they did at that particular juncture. To increase the rates of seigniorage was one thing, but to raise the revenue of the tax was quite another. Increased rates would result in larger revenue only if the volume of activity at the mint did not decrease proportionately. However, as already explained, the State had no direct control over the volume of activity at the mint. But the authorities knew that if they devalued the currency, a high level of minting activity would follow as speculators rushed to take advantage of the gap between the nominal value of the money and its lowered metallic content. Therefore the ideal moment to raise the seigniorage, if one wanted to do so, was indeed the time of a devaluation. The Florentine authorities showed themselves well acquainted with such niceties. In 1347, in the same ordinance in which they decreed the devaluation of the silver currency, they made provisions for a drastic increase of the seigniorage. Before 1347 the charges levied were 1.41 percent for the *grosso* and 5.74 percent for the *quattrino*. The provision of July 1347 raised the seigniorage to 4.62 percent for the *grosso* and 6.60 percent for the *quattrino*.

[27]G. Pinto, *Il libro del Biadaiolo: carestie e annona a Firenze dalla metà del Duecento al 1348* (Florence, 1978), p. 100.

[28]*Ibid.*

Because the purpose of the move was not to raise reimbursement to the mint but to guarantee greater revenues for the Commune, the new provision made clear that of the 4.62 percent levied on the *grossi*, 3.42 percent was to go to the Commune's treasury; similarly, of the 6.60 percent levied on the *quattrini*, the Commune was to expect 1.90 percent.[29]

It is worth noticing that, in the ordinance in which they decreed both the raise of the seigniorage and the devaluation of the silver currency, the monetary authorities emphasized the fiscal reasons for the measures, giving preeminence to the seigniorage question and presenting the devaluation almost as a support measure to increase the revenues of the Commune.[30] Giovanni Villani, in his Chronicle, emphasized instead the devaluation and presented it as the outcome of the lobbying of the clothiers, who feared a weakening of the florin.[31] As Oscar Wilde once said, truth is rarely pure and never simple.

On the whole, the monetary authorities of Florence had managed fairly well. The Florentine *lira* emerged from the gold crisis of 1345–1347 devalued by less than 30 percent, that is, by about 30 percent if one refers to the *grosso*, by about 20 percent if one refers to the *quattrino*, and by nothing if one refers to the *denaro* (see Appendix, Table D). Considering that the value of silver had risen 30 percent on the market in relation to gold, and that the mint had had to find ways to in-

[29]Bernocchi, *Le monete*, vol. 1, p. 97. See also the documents reproduced therein, pp. 93–96.

[30]Bernocchi, *Le monete*, vol. 1, pp. 97ff.

[31]G. Villani, *Cronica* XII, 97.

crease its contribution to the Commune's treasury during the famine of 1347, one must conclude that the financial authorities managed to keep the situation under control. Those who had everything to gain from a rise in the rate of the florin and everything to lose from its fall undoubtedly put pressure on the government in favor of the devaluation, as the chroniclers relate. But they did not overdo it—or were not in the position to. The devaluation of the silver currency was kept within the amount strictly necessary to avoid a dangerous fall of the florin and maintain stability. That there was resistance to devaluation is shown also by the fact that in both 1345 and 1347 the authorities devalued only (or principally) the coins that were the main target of speculation at the cost of breaking the alignment between the various kinds of coins.

CHAPTER III

High Consumption and Financial Speculation: 1350 to 1370

THE DEVALUATIONS of 1345 and 1347 staved off the deflationary effects of the rise in the value of silver, but the crisis continued. A substantial body of wealth had been destroyed both through the fall in value of shares in the public debt and through the bankruptcies of the companies. The prestige Florence held in the international market had suffered a severe blow. Credit was difficult to obtain; the public debt, the interest rates, and unemployment were alarmingly high; wages, rents, and the prices of nonagricultural products were painfully depressed.

It was against this background that, in the summer of 1348, the Black Death broke out. In a few months the city's population was cut almost in half: from some eighty thousand to some forty-five thousand inhabitants.[1] The surrounding countryside suffered proportionately.

[1]A. Falsini, "Firenze dopo il 1348: le conseguenze della peste nera," *Archivio storico italiano* 129 (1971), p. 436; Ch. M. de la Roncière, *Florence centre économique régional au XIVe siècle*, vol. 2 (Aix-en-Provence, 1976), p. 696.

In human terms, the plague was an unmitigated disaster. In terms of the economy, its effects were far from being disastrous. The plague in essence broke the vicious spiral of deflation. Since the number of *capita* was suddenly and dramatically reduced, the average *per capita* amount of currency available rose. In addition, during the three years that followed the plague, the output of the mint remained high.[2] Consequently, cash balances were unusually large, and they were not hoarded: the prevailing mood among the survivors was that of spending. Thus prices and wages increased. Matteo Villani, who witnessed the events, made the following comment:

> the greater part of things were worth twice as much and more than they used to be before the said mortal-

[2]In the half-year May-October 1348, only 5,000 gold florins were coined, and the value of the combined minting of *grossi* and *quattrini* went down to 28,000 *lire* in comparison with 493,000 *lire* of the preceding six months. But with the following year, the mint's output returned to its previous high levels.

The years 1347–1351 stand out as a homogeneous, coherent period of high minting activity. Between May 1347 and April 1351, the Florentine mint issued more than 865,000 gold florins worth over 2,800,000 lire, in addition to *grossi* and *quattrini* for the respective amounts of over 1,000,000 and about 146,000 *lire*.

There seems to have been, however, a change in the structure of the demand for money in the aftermath of the plague. Data on the mint's output are significant in this respect. Beteen May 1349 and April 1351, the issues of *grossi* continued to increase (from 137,000 *lire* in the half-year May-October 1349, to 302,000 *lire* in the half-year November 1350-April 1351) while the issues of *quattrini* continued to decrease. The phenomenon must be related to the contemporaneous increase in prices and wages. At the level of post-plague prices, a *grosso* bought a chicken or two dozen eggs and ten *grossi* were the equivalent of a laborer's wage for five working days.

See M. Bernocchi, *Le monete della repubblica fiorentina*, vol. 3 (Florence, 1974–1978), pp. 67 and 252; de la Roncière, *Florence*, vol. 2, p. 521 and vol. 4, p. 116, n. 86.

ity. And the [cost of] labor and manufacture in all kinds of crafts and trades rose inordinately to more than twice the usual.[3]

The painstaking research of a French scholar fully confirms Matteo Villani's testimony. According to de la Roncière's findings, nominal wages in Florence increased, as the following figures show (using the average for the years 1326–1347 as the base for the index numbers):[4]

	Masons	Laborers	Gardeners	Weavers
1326–1347	100	100	100	100
1350–1356	232	289	218	273

Prices of goods increased in a less uniform manner, but on the whole they grew less than wages.[5] Real wages therefore increased, thus reflecting the relative scarcity of labor as a factor of production.

The quotation of the florin remained stable between 60 and 63 soldi until 1350. In the spring of that year, however, the market of precious metals saw the reversal of the trend that had prevailed over the previous decade. Silver became more and more abundant, and its price began to drop in terms of gold. Contemporary documents are quite explicit. On March 13, 1350, it was recorded in Siena that there was "great abundance of silver." Seven days later, in Florence, it was noticed that "there is abundance of silver, whose price is falling." On April 8, a Venetian document reported that "silver is

[3]M. Villani, *Cronica di Matteo Villani*, F. Dragomanni, ed. (Florence, 1846), I, 5.

[4]De la Roncière, *Florence*, vol. 1, p. 390.

[5]De la Roncière, *Florence*, vol. 1, p. 264.

multiplying."[6] The revaluation of gold had nothing to do with the plague, but it caused the quotation of the florin to move from 60–63 *soldi* in 1350 to 68–70 *soldi* in 1355.[7] Thus in the Florence of 1351 prices, wages, and the quotation of the florin were all rising. Only rents, for obvious demographic reasons, remained depressed. Deflation had given way to inflation.

The effects of the new developments were soon felt at the mint. In January 1351, the monetary authorities complained that the rise in the cost of labor and in the price of coal had reduced the profits of the mint to "next to nothing" (*quasi nichil*). Under the pressure of, and with the excuse of, such circumstances, the authorities proceeded to increase the seigniorage on the minting of silver. On January 25, 1351, the seigniorage on the *grosso* was raised from 4.62 to 5.98 percent. About two months later, on March 13, the seigniorage on the *quattrino* was increased from 6.60 to 15.09 percent.[8] The operation rested on the assumption that the demand for new silver money was inelastic with respect to the price of the minting service. The assumption proved to be wrong. In April 1351, the authorities complained that silver no longer flowed into the mint,[9] and the data on the mint's output confirm their

[6]For Siena, see D. Promis, *Monete della repubblica di Siena* (Turin, 1868), p. 79, doc. 3; for Florence, see de la Roncière, *Florence*, vol. 4, p. 114, n. 81; for Venice, see R. Cessi, *Problemi monetari veneziani* (Padua, 1937), p. 99, doc. 111.

[7]De la Roncière, *Florence*, vol. 4, pp. 499ff; Bernocchi, *Le monete*, vol. 3, p. 79; C. M. Cipolla, *Studi di storia della moneta: i movimenti dei cambi in Italia dal secolo XII al secolo XV* (Pavia, 1948), p. 60.

[8]Bernocchi, *Le monete*, vol. 1, pp. 118–123.

[9]Bernocchi, *Le monete*, vol. 1, p. 126.

complaints.[10] The authorities were forced to retreat. They brought down the seigniorage but their new ordinance was purposely ambiguous: it made reference only to the previous increase of the seigniorage for the *grossi,* and it seemed to imply that the seigniorage had to be reduced for the *grossi* and not for the *quattrini.*[11]

The discrimination against the *quattrino* is significant. The economic trends that prevailed after the plague of 1348 and the repeal in October 1350 of the provision that had reduced the number of lower guilds had strengthened the position of artisans and shopkeepers (that is, the *Arti Minori*) within the administration. These groups saw in the growing quantity of *quattrini* in circulation one of the reasons for the weakening of the petty currency. The fact that the quotation of the florin had started to rise again must have alarmed them, and it is not at all absurd to hint that they resisted a reduction of the high seigniorage on the *quattrino* in order to penalize the minting of this coin. If this analysis is correct, one should view the events of the spring of 1351 as a prelude to the monetary policy that the *Arti Minori* were to proclaim about thirty years later, at the time of the Ciompi revolt.[12]

In all likelihood, the volume of coinage would have shrunk even if the seigniorage charges on silver coins had not been increased. This is suggested by the fact that the issues of florins also collapsed and yet the seigniorage on the florins had not been raised. Clearly

[10]See below, p. 52.

[11]This is in fact how the ordinance has been interpreted by Bernocchi, *Le monete,* vol. 3, p. 198.

[12]See below, Chapt. IV.

other and more general economic factors were at play. Although at present we do not know what these factors were, we do know that between mid-1351 and mid-1352 the combined output of the mint dropped by 90 percent, as shown by the following figures:[13]

VALUE OF MINTINGS (IN THOUSANDS
OF LIRE DI DENARI PICCIOLI)

Period	florins	grossi	quattrini	total
November 1350–April 1351	657.8	301.6	1.9	961.3
May 1351–October 1351	260.7	190.4	6.3	457.4
November 1351–April 1352	85.5	8.7	.5	94.7

Once the mint's output had fallen, it remained at a very depressed level for almost twenty years. The production of florins declined from over 250,000 pieces per year between 1344 and 1351 to an average of less than 30,000 pieces per year, with a slight downward trend throughout the period 1355–1369 (see Figure 1). Even more dramatic the new phase appeared in relation to the silver currency. No *quattrini* at all were coined between April 1352 and January 1372. *Grossi* were not issued between November 1353 and April 1359, and after that date only a very limited number were minted.[14]

The contraction of the mint's output, combined with

[13]On the mint's output, see Bernocchi, *Le monete*, vol. 3, pp. 67 and 252. The value of the output of florins was calculated on the basis of the average quotation for the florin, derived from de la Roncière, *Florence*, vol. 4, pp. 498ff.

[14]Bernocchi, *Le monete*, vol. 3, pp. 67–68 and 252–253. Only in the six-month period May-October 1359, there was an issue of *quattrini* for which the amount is not known: see Bernocchi, *Le monete*, vol. 1, pp. 134–135.

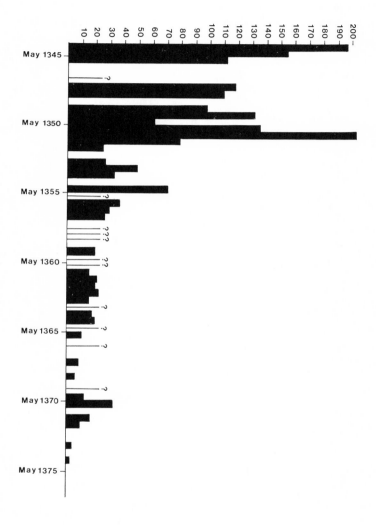

Fig. 1. Number of gold florins issued by the mint of Florence 1366–1375

the metallic stability of the silver currency, (the two phenomena were obviously related) could not fail to affect the movements of prices, wages, and the quotation of gold. Prices and wages stopped growing in the course of 1353, and from 1354 until 1369 showed a remarkable tendency toward stability.[15] The gold florin continued to strengthen until 1355 and then stabilized within the range of 65 to 70 *soldi*, the most common quotations being those between 67 and 69 *soldi*.[16] Thus, between 1355 and 1369, Florence came to enjoy a long phase of stable prices, stable wages, and stable quotations of gold, on the backdrop of a stable silver currency and a reduced output from the mint.

The essential stability of prices and nominal wages actually meant the continuation of the high (for those times) real wages that had been reached in the years immediately following the plague. De la Roncière rightly defined the twenty years between 1350 and 1369 as a time of "fat cattle" for Florentine workers.[17] But although those twenty years were good for the workers, one must beware of concluding that they were years of "fat cattle" for the Florentine economy taken as a whole—far from it. There was not indeed the collapse that was supposed when it was thought that Florentine wool production had dropped from about 79,000 rolls of woolen cloth in 1339 to less than

[15]De la Roncière, *Florence*, vol. 1. Also contributing to the stability of the period was the fact that during these years crops were generally good.

[16]De la Roncière, *Florence*, vol. 4, pp. 499ff.; Bernocchi, *Le monete*, vol. 3, p. 79; Cipolla, *Studi*, p. 60.

[17]De la Roncière, *Florence*, vol. 1, pp. 494–496 and de la Roncière, *La condition des salariés à Florence*, p. 24.

20,000 in 1382.[18] These figures have been challenged, and today it is thought that "the volume of wool production in Florence fluctuated approximately between 20,000 and 30,000 rolls throughout the fourteenth century."[19] In the twenty years following the plague, the Florentine economy proved to be remarkably resilient. In 1369, at least 108 trade companies were still active in Florence.[20] However, the days of expansion were now only a memory. The growth of Florence between 1250 and 1320 had been based on abundant, cheap, and for those times highly productive labor; on interest rates that were reasonable for the times; and on a quotation of the florin in terms of petty currency that grew on average by 4 percent annually for about seventy years, with the expansionary effects already explained.

All these factors vanished with the 1330s and the 1340s. The two decades that followed (1350–1370) were not tragic like the 1340s, but if they were years of "fat cattle" for some people, for others they were a time of difficulties. In some ways the period of 1350–1369 was one of contradictions. Let us try to analyze it more closely.

We have already seen that the plague was followed by a rise in both prices and wages, with wages leading prices. Throughout the period (1350–1369), we have

[18]R. Davidsohn, "Blüte und Niedergang der Florentiner Tuchindustrie," *Zeitschrift für der gesamte Staatswissenschaft* 85 (1978).

[19]H. Hoshino, "Per la storia dell'arte della lana," pp. 61ff and 80. See also H. Hoshino, *L'arte della lana in Firenze nel basso Medioevo* (Florence, 1980), chaps. 1–3.

[20]P. Silva, "L'ultimo trattato commerciale tra Pisa e Firenze," *Studi storici del Crivellucci* 17 (1909), p. 658.

seen that real wages remained exceptionally high. In itself this was no problem. The problem was that the appreciably higher cost of labor was not compensated for by higher labor productivity—on the contrary. An indication of the difficult situation that prevailed in the labor market after the plague can be found at the mint itself, which was a business like any other, operated with a view to profit.

After the plague the mint was short of both technicians and unskilled labor, because of the high mortality among its workers.[21] The vacancies were filled, though not without difficulty,[22] but that only meant the substitution of one problem with another. Now workers not only demanded increasingly higher wages—they also demanded to work shorter hours. On January 13, 1351, the mint's officers reported a series of strikes.[23] A few days later, they announced that a certain Simon Dante from Maiano, who had once worked at the mint, kept coming to it and inciting the workers to abstain from working.[24] As time went on, the situation grew more tense. In 1365, the directors of the mint exploded: "the four workers will not work except at their convenience, and if they are remonstrated with, they reply with rude and arrogant words saying they will not work except when it suits them and on condition that their wages are increased. And although offers of reasonable wages

[21]Falsini, *Firenze dopo il 1348*, p. 441.

[22]A document of the mint dated January 25, 1351, speaks of "carestia laborantium" ("shortage of workers"). Cf. Bernocchi, *Le monete*, vol. 1, p. 118.

[23]"Ipsi overerii, adirictatores et moneterii sepe concorditer se absentant et laborare recusant in dicta cecha contra voluntatem dominorum monete." Cf. Bernocchi, *Le monete*, vol. 1, pp. 115–116.

[24]Bernocchi, *Le monete*, vol. 1, p. 119.

have been made many times to them, they behave even worse, still increasing in arrogance, and pretend that none other than themselves shall come to work in the mint, threatening anyone who dares to overcome their obstruction; thus they conspire inside the mint."[25] This passage undoubtedly reflects the employer's point of view, but the substance of the argument can hardly be denied. As we have already seen, the increases in the costs of labor had reduced the mint's profits to "next to nothing," so much so that in 1351 the mint was forced to increase the seigniorage on the coinage of silver money.

There is no reason to suppose that the events at the mint did not have their counterpart in other businesses in Florence. The mint workers were not exceptional; Matteo Villani recorded that after the plague "the lower classes, both men and women, were not willing to work at their usual trades."[26] All forms of labor became more expensive, whether that of journeymen, craftsmen working in their workshops, or people working at home for the putting-out system. The efforts of the clothiers to resist the growing demands of the dyers are significant in this connection.[27]

If the cost of labor was unusually high, so was the cost of money. As we shall see later, the continual and pressing demand for funds from the government

[25]Bernocchi, Le monete, vol. 1, p. 142 (document dated January 30, 1365).

[26]M. Villani, Cronica I, 4.

[27]A. Doren, Die Florentine Wollentuchindustrie vom XIV bis zum XVI Jahrhundert: Studien aus der Florentiner Wirtschaftsgeschichte (Stuttgart, 1901), vol. 1, pp. 300–302; N. Rodolico, Il popolo minuto (Bologna, 1889), docs. 26 and 27; G. A. Brucker, Florentine Politics and Society (1343–1378) (Princeton, 1962), p. 195.

kept interest rates at a high level. The combination of high costs of both labor and money at a time when the international economic scene was depressed and the florin was weak must have reduced the profitability of big and medium-sized manufacturing enterprises. Meanwhile, because of the demographic situation, rents remained depressed,[28] and the combination of high wages and low rents squeezed the profits of the landowners.

However, not all sectors of the economy suffered: the picture was extremely complex. The high level of real wages in the perid 1350–1369 stimulated consumption—a fact well documented by the sources.[29] Thus the workers' "fat years" must have been years of "fat cattle" for the shopkeepers too. Similarly, the high rewards for labor certainly spelled prosperity for those craftsmen who did not rely on hired workers, or only did so on a very small scale.

The new price structure and the resulting new hierarchy of profitability strengthened the position of the *Arti Minori* (essentially the artisans and shopkeepers) as opposed to the *Arti Maggiori*. The 1350s and 1360s saw the economic, social, and political rise of a whole class of "new people": people who came "this one

[28]D. Herlihy, "Santa Maria Impruneta: a rural commune in the late Middle Ages," in *Florentine Studies*, N. Rubinstein, ed. (Evanston, 1968), pp. 273–274; G. Pinto, "Forme di conduzione e rendita fondiaria nel contado fiorentino (secoli XIV e XV): le terre dell'ospedale di San Gallo," in *Studi di storia medievale e moderna per Ernesto Sestan* (Florence, 1980), pp. 315ff; A. Sapori, "Pigioni di case e botteghe a Firenze nel Trecento," in *Studi di storia economica* (Florence, 1955), pp. 388–389.

[29]The contemporary statement of M. Villani, *Cronica* I, 4 and III, 56 is fully confirmed by the detailed research of de la Roncière, *Florence*, vol. 1.

from Capalle, that one from Cilicciavole, and the other from Sugame or Viminiccio," as Boccaccio playfully wrote,[30] or "middle people," according to another writer,[31] but in any case people who succeeded in climbing the social ladder, inducing Matteo Villani to comment in a supercilious tone that "the direction and government of the city of Florence came in no small part into [the hands of] men recently arrived from the countryside and districts of Florence, little skilled in civic needs."[32]

The "new people" had neither the experience nor the vision of the old oligarchy of Florentine business-men. Their cultural horizons and ambitions were more limited, and it is not surprising that the increased fi-nancial weight of these parvenus affected the structure of investment in the Florentine economy after 1350. In addition, the objective conditions in the market favored a redirection of capital.

The public budget was continually in desperate need of money. To meet this need, the authorities tradition-ally favored loans over new taxes, but it was not easy to obtain additional loans. The ordinance of 1345 fixing the maximum interest on public loans at 5 percent was still in force. It was an unrealistic limitation, for rates of over 15 percent prevailed on the market. To circumvent the difficulty, it was decided in 1358 to authorize the unorthodox registration of loans as being three times the amount actually subscribed. This, together with the highly volatile price of shares, offered excellent oppor-

[30]F. Corazzini, *Le lettere edite e inedite di messer Giovanni Boccaccio* (Florence, 1877), p. 74.

[31]Quoted by Brucker, *Florentine Politics*, p. 53.

[32]M. Villani, *Cronica* X, 65.

tunities for investment for anyone with ready cash: speculation on public loans and related shares produced returns worthy of the title of usury.

Faced with high risks and reduced profits in the mercantile-manufacturing sector and low risk and high profit in the area of financial investment and speculation, capital understandably shifted into the latter.[33] Matteo Villani, who knew the situation first hand, made a comment that, apart from its moralistic tone, puts the matter in a nutshell: "not charity or affection for the republic, but cupidity for the huge profit, has drawn many away from trade into usury [namely high interest loans to the government] against the good and habitual custom of our fathers."[34] "From trade into usury," that is, from production to speculation: this was one of the main traits of the age.

The other main trait I have already alluded to, but it is important to return to it. Matteo Villani wrote that since "everybody made much money by their trades and earned inordinate amounts . . . the mass of the people were ready to buy and consume the best things and would pay more, competing with people of higher station: a thing which is both deplorable and extraordinary to recount and yet is continually observed. . . . And thus the populace feast and dine and dress and entertain as if in the midst of the most extraordinary

[33]Cf. A. Sapori, "L'interesse del denaro a Firenze," in *Studi di Storia Economica* (Florence, 1955); A. Sapori, "Pigioni di case e botteghe"; Brucker, *Florentine Politics*, p. 20 and *passim*; M. Becker, *Florence in Transition* (Baltimore, 1967–1968), pp. 219ff and *passim*; and particularly R. Barducci, "Politica e speculazione finanziaria a Firenze dopo la crisi del primo Trecento (1343–1358)," *Archivio storico italiano* 137 (1979).

[34]M. Villani, *Cronica* VIII, 71.

abundance."[35] The phenomenon was not limited to Florence. After all, the plague had made labor scarce all over Europe. Not far away from Florence, in Piacenza, the chronicler Giovanni de Mussis made similar comments on the unusually high standards of living prevalent in his city and remarked that those who spent freely were "not only the nobles and the merchants but also those who practice manual trades, who make reckless purchases, especially on clothes for themselves and their wives: employment seems to provide them with enough to support all this."[36]

In Florence, however, it was not only private consumption that stood at very high levels. The heavy borrowing on the part of the Commune served to pay for public consumption. Whether one looks at the public or at the private sector, one distinctly feels that in Florence the decades that followed the Black Death were characterized by a high level of consumption and a depressed level of productive investment, which is not inconsistent with the other impression that the period in question was one of relatively widespread wellbeing in the presence of economic stagnation.[37]

[35]M. Villani, *Cronica* III, 56.

[36]G. de Mussis, "Chronicon placentinum," *Rerum italicarum scriptores*, vol. 16, cols. 582–584.

[37]M. Becker ("Problemi della finanza pubblica fiorentina della seconda metà del Trecento e dei primi del Quattrocento," *Archivio storico italiano* 123 [1965], p. 440) notices that in the 1360s the yield of the "gabelle" was noticeably higher than in the previous decades and concludes that the economy was "expanding." It should be pointed out that, first, a part of the increase was due to an increase in the rate of taxation (cf. Ch. M. de la Roncière, "Indirect Taxes or 'gabelles' at Florence in the Fourteenth Century," in *Florentine Studies*, N. Rubinstein, ed. [Evanston, 1968], p. 171n) and, second, the yield of the taxes considered was related more to consumption than to the gross product.

CHAPTER IV

The Affair of the *Quattrini*

I

In 1683, the "monetarist economist" Geminiano Montanari wrote that "often monetary devaluations cannot
be blamed on local rulers but on the neighboring states:
it is very difficult to prevent this disease from spread-
ing like the plague from one state to another."[1] It is
indeed true that a devaluation could easily set off an
international chain reaction of related devaluations in
neighboring states, not only because of international
competitiveness, but also because individual states enjoyed only limited monetary sovereignty and within
their boundaries foreign coins circulated in large numbers. This must be kept in mind if one wants to understand what happened in Florence in the 1360s.

As I have explained already, the volume of minting
depended on private individuals bringing metal to the
mint to be transformed into coins. In the case of the

[1]G. Montanari, "La zecca in Consulta di Stato (1683)," in *Economisti del Cinque e Seicento*, A. Graziani, ed. (Bari, 1913), p. 348.

63

petty currency (though not in the case of the gold currency),[2] people had it minted mostly if and when they would profit from a difference between the exchange value of the coins and the value of their metallic content. The mechanism was the following. When the authorities decreed a reduction of the silver content of petty coins, people brought silver (also in the form of old coins) to the mint. Inevitably, as recoinage progressed, the gap between face value and intrinsic value became progressively smaller. When it came close to the seigniorage charges, minting came to a halt. If the authorities wanted to sustain additional output of currency, they had to have recourse to further reductions. If instead they wanted to keep the metallic content of the currency stable, they had to resign themselves to seeing its output practically halted.

This, however, was not the whole story. Periods of mint inactivity, such as occurred in Florence after 1351, actually encouraged the importation of foreign coins, the phenomenon being favored by two circumstances: first, the small, territorial scale of Italian states caused most of the trade to be international in character, and, second, neighboring states minted coins that were very similar, both in design and metallic content, the similarity often being the result of specific monetary agreements. Gresham's law then made sure that when foreign coins infiltrated a given state, they were normally of lower metallic content than the local currency. Thus

[2]One of the reasons for the difference was that the gold currency was the favorite form of storing value, whereas nobody wanted to hold and hoard petty coins. Another reason was that the seigniorage for the florin amounted to only 0.6 percent, whereas that for the *quattrino* was more than ten times higher and that for the *denaro* more than thirty times higher.

the Italian states found themselves faced with an insoluble dilemma: if they wanted to mint petty currency, they had to debase it in order to make it worthwhile for private citizens to bring metal to the mint; if they did not devalue, issues stopped and the vacuum was filled by an influx of foreign petty currency that was weaker than the local money.

Florence in the 1360s was a prime example of the way this mechanism worked. The minting of *grossi* and *quattrini* ceased after 1351: as the authorities refused to further reduce the metallic content of the currency, nobody brought metal to the mint to receive coins for which they had to pay a high seigniorage. As time went on, petty currency from neighboring states began to infiltrate the Florentine market more and more, filling the gap created by the mint's inactivity. In 1366 the Florentine authorities reported that the city was being invaded by weaker *denari* from "neighboring and nearby places," and that this invasion had led to the disappearance of the local *denaro*.[3] The vagueness of the designation "neighboring and nearby places" had a diplomatic *raison-d'etre*, but the rest of the story shows that the money invading the Florentine market place from "neighboring and nearby places" was mainly Pisan.

Pisan currency had a metallic parity weaker than the Florentine, but, given the different alignment between the various denominations in the two systems, the difference between Pisan and Florentine money varied according to the denomination considered.[4] In 1366 it seems that the largest difference was in the *denaro picci-*

---

[3]M. Bernocchi, *Le monete della repubblica fiorentina*, vol. 1 (Florence, 1974–1978), p. 150.

[4]See below, n. 17.

olo, for the *denaro* circulating at the time was still the one struck in 1331, which had not been affected by the devaluations of 1345 and 1347. With its anachronistic metallic content, even when worn, the *denaro picciolo* was the most obvious coin to be exposed to the competition of the "bad money" from abroad.[5]

This is consistent with the report by the Florentine authorities in 1366 that the invasion of weak foreign currency consisted mainly of *denari*. To halt the invasion, the authorities acted on June 22, 1366. Symbolically, they banned all foreign petty currency from the Florentine territory, but they were fully aware that such bans were of no practical value and that the only way to stop the invasion of the foreign "bad" money was to devalue the local currency. Thus in the same ordinance the authorities ordered the minting of a new *denaro* with a content of 0.0337 grams of pure silver. In relation to the theoretical content of the *denaro* of 1331 (0.0524 grams), this represented a considerable deval-

---

[5]The *denaro* of Florence in circulation in 1366 was still the one coined in 1331 and the years immediately following. With a theoretical metallic content of 0.0524 grams of pure silver, it was out of line in relation to the other coins issued after the debasements of 1345–1347. In fact during the period 1348–1365 a Florentine *lira* had the following theoretical equivalents:

11.12 grams of pure silver when paid in (4) *grossi*;
10.68 grams of pure silver when paid in (60) *quattrini*; and
12.58 grams of pure silver when paid in (240) *denari*.

Thus the *denaro* contained proportionately more silver with respect to its face value than did its multiples. At its face value the *denaro* was therefore undervalued in relation to the *quattrino* and the *grosso* (without taking into account the higher costs of minting it). This explains why no more were minted even during the period of 1347–1351 when the volume of output of all other types of currency at the Florence mint was very high.

uation—of about 36 percent. But 20 to 30 percent of it was bringing the *denaro* into line with the *grosso* and the *quattrino*, thus making up for what had not been done in 1345 and 1347. In relation to the prevailing silver parity of the *lira* as determined by the current *grossi* and *quattrini*, there was only a further 10 to 20 percent debasement intended to counteract and check the impact of the Pisan *denaro*.[6]

The way the operation of 1366 was carried out clearly reveals the authorities' concern to limit the devaluation to a bare minimum. The Florentine *denaro* was issued with a metallic content still considerably higher than that of the corresponding Pisan coin, and the two other silver coins, the *quattrino* and the *grosso*, which were also threatened by the foreign currency, were left intact.

Diverted by the debasement of the *denaro*, speculation inevitably moved to the *quattrini* and *grossi*. In December 1367, the artisans of Florence complained of an invasion of Pisan *quattrini* that, although weaker in silver content than the Florentine *quattrini*, were being exchanged in Florence at the same face value as the latter (four *denari*). The artisans petitioned that the foreign *quattrini* should not be allowed to be valued in

[6]As usual after a debasement, private individuals took silver to the mint to profit from the operation. Between May and October 1366, 579,600 *denari* were coined, and another 478,800 pieces were minted in the six-month period from May to October 1367. These were essentially modest amounts (the equivalents respectively of 2,415 and 1,995 lire) that the market was easily able to absorb, witness the quotation of the florin which remained stable. Gaps in documents prevent us from knowing whether *denari* were minted in the periods November 1366-April 1367 and November 1367-April 1368. Cf. Bernocchi, *Le monete*, vol. 3, p. 253.

Florence for more than three Florentine *denari*.[7] A few months later, in July 1368, the Florentine authorities denounced that neighboring Communes were minting inferior *grossi* that were driving the Florentine *grossi* out of the market.[8] At this juncture it was decided to intervene and protect the *grosso*. The only defense possible was devaluation, but the Florentine authorities were obstinately reluctant to devaluate. So they sought a compromise. The Florentine *grosso* then in circulation had a face value of five *soldi*. This *grosso* was left intact. Instead, an old coin that had not been minted since 1306 was resuscitated: the *grosso* of two *soldi*. In July 1368, the mint was authorized to issue a new *grosso* of two *soldi* with a metallic content of 1.084 grams of pure silver. The *grosso* then circulating in Pisa was also worth two *soldi* and had a silver content of 1.056 grams.[9] The Florentine authorities were clearly guided by two considerations: to narrow as much as possible the gap between Florentine and Pisan currencies, and to mask the devaluation by using a coin that had not been issued for quite a long time.

However, the maneuver was ill conceived and was destined to fail. The *grosso* of five *soldi* in circulation

[7]Ch. M. de la Roncière, *Florence centre économique regional au XIVe siècle*, vol. 4 (Aix-en-Provence, 1976), p. 108, n. 44. The rate the Florentine artisans proposed implied a reduction in the nominal value of the Pisan *quattrino* of 25 percent. It seems (see below, n. 17) that the metallic content of the Pisan *quattrino* (0.146 grams of pure silver) was inferior by only 18 percent to the *quattrino* of Florence (0.178 grams of pure silver). However, the figures agree in order of magnitude, particularly if one considers that the rate proposed by the Florentine artisans probably represented a rounded-off figure.

[8]Bernocchi, *Le monete*, vol. 1, p. 156.

[9]See below, n. 17.

before 1368 had a silver content of 2.78 grams, which meant that a Florentine *lira* (20 *soldi*) paid for by four of these *grossi* had a theoretical equivalent of 11.12 grams of pure silver. The *grosso* of two *soldi* issued in 1368 had a silver content of 1.084 grams, whereby a Florentine *lira* paid for in ten of these *grossi* had a theoretical equivalent of 10.84 grams. A debasement of only 2.5 percent had taken place; but the 2.5 percent difference was enough to threaten the *grosso* of five *soldi*, which was already under pressure from the weaker foreign *grossi* and which now had also to face the competition of a new local *grosso* in relation to which it was undervalued. If the purpose of the Florentine action was to end the speculative melting down of the *grossi* of five *soldi*, the outcome of the action must have been exactly the opposite.

The authorities soon realized that they had made a mistake. To save the *grosso* of five *soldi* from complete extinction they had to devalue it, however reluctantly. This they did at the middle of 1369, reducing its silver content by 2.5 percent and thus bringing it to parity with the *grosso* of two *soldi*.[10]

In all this maneuvering the authorities were careful to leave the *quattrino* alone. Nevertheless, as the pro-

[10] The metallic content of the *grosso* of 5 *soldi* was lowered from 2.78 grams of pure silver to 2.71 grams. Therefore one *lira* paid for by 4 of these *grossi* had a theoretical equivalent of 10.84 grams, which was exactly equal to a *lira* paid for by 10 *grossi* of 2 *soldi* (each *grosso* of 2 *soldi* containing 1.084 grams of pure silver).

The Pisan *grosso* of 2 *soldi* contained 1.056 grams of silver; therefore one *lira* when paid for with 10 Pisan *grossi* had the theoretical equivalent of 10.56 grams of pure silver. Consequently, after the Florentine devaluation of 1368–1369, the difference between Pisan and Florentine currency at the level of the *grosso* had been reduced to less than 3 percent.

test of the artisans in 1367 proves,[11] the *quattrino* was under great pressure from its Pisan counterpart. The Florentines' inaction was due neither to lack of interest nor to negligence. They had decided to debase the *denaro*, thinking, and rightly so, that its role in the monetary system of Florence was marginal.[12] They debased the *grosso* of five *soldi* only after desperately trying to protect it, and in any case they were able to limit the debasement to a mere 2.5 percent, because the Florentine *grosso* was not much stronger than the Pisan.[13] In the case of the *quattrino*, the position was very different: in order to protect it from the pressure of its Pisan counterpart its devaluation would have to be substantial, because the Pisan *quattrino* was weaker than the Florentine by a good 18 percent.[14] Moreover, with the *denaro* confined to a marginal role, the *quattrino* had become the principal denomination on which the local monetary system, and thus the structure of internal prices, was based. To touch the *quattrino* would mean endangering the comfortable monetary stability that had prevailed since the beginning of the 1350s and to which the ruling administration was totally committed.

But the Florentines were trapped. Having taken steps to protect first the *denaro* and then the *grosso*, they had unwittingly ended by leaving exposed the very currency they most wished to save—the *quattrino*. One should add that in 1370 Florence and Pisa signed a

[11]See above, pp. 42, 66.

[12]About 1360, one *denaro* was the equivalent of 0.83 percent of a laborer's daily wage. .

[13]See above, n. 10.

[14]The Florentine *quattrino* had a metallic content of 0.178 grams of pure silver, whereas the Pisan *quattrino* had a metallic content of 0.146 grams of pure silver. See below, n. 17.

commercial treaty that was intended to strengthen the business relations between the two cities[15] and that would hence increase the pressure of the weaker Pisan money on the Florentine currency.

During 1370 and 1371, Florence was invaded by a significant amount of petty foreign currency. As a document of the times puts it, "much bad money is brought in very great quantity into the city of Florence."[16] The influx seems to have consisted chiefly of *quattrini* and *denari*, which is not surprising. Since the *quattrino* had not been touched either in 1366 or in 1368–1369, the difference between its metallic content and that of the corresponding Pisan money was quite high. As for the *denaro*, the reader will remember that it had been reduced in 1366, but, because of the concern to keep debasement to a minimum, its metallic content had been kept at a level still considerably higher than its Pisan counterpart. In numerical terms, before October 1371 the theoretical silver content of the Pisan currency was lower than that of Florentine money by 2.6 percent for the *grosso*, 18 percent for the *quattrino*, and 27 percent for the *denaro*.[17]

On September 6, 1371, under the pressure of events, a special commission was appointed in Florence to study methods of blocking the influx of foreign currency and to suggest a new metallic content for the

[15]P. Silva, "L'ultimo trattato commerciale tra Pisa e Firenze," *Studi storici del Crivellucci* 17 (1909).

[16]De la Roncière, *Florence*, vol. 4, p. 118, n. 100.

[17]On the silver equivalent of the Florentine *lira*, see Appendix, Table D. The silver equivalent of the Pisan *lira* has been estimated on the basis of the information contained in a Pisan document of August 1371, published by P. Silva ("Il governo di Pietra Gambacorta in Pisa e le sue relazioni col resto della Toscana e coi Visconti," *Annali della*

Florentine *quattrino* and *denaro* that would protect the coins from their "bad" foreign counterparts.[18] At this

R. Scuola Normale Superiore di Pisa: classe di filosofia e filologia 23 [1912], p. 128, n. 2). The document is summarized in the accompanying table.

Coin	Fineness in -/1000	Grams of pure silver in 1 lb.* of alloy	Coins struck from 1 lb. of alloy	Grams of pure silver in each coin
grosso of 2 *soldi*	958.3	325.34	308	1.056
quattrino	145.83	49.51	339	0.146
denaro	41.67	14.15	576	0.0246

*1 lb. = 339.5 grams

It follows that one Pisan *lira* corresponded to

10.56 grams of pure silver when paid in (10) *grossi*;
8.76 grams of pure silver when paid in (60) *quattrini*;
5.90 grams of pure silver when paid in (240) *denari*.

These conclusions do not agree with the conclusions reached by Silva who misinterpreted the document. He concluded that "one *lira* of Pisan *moneta grossa* of copper was worth 28 *soldi* and 3 *denari* and one *lira* of petty currency was worth 48 *soldi*" (Silva, *loc. cit.*, p. 129), but the document in question does not say this at all. It states that from one pound (weight) of specific fineness (145.83/1000) were to be struck 28 *soldi* and 3 *denari* of *quattrini* and from one pound (weight) of specific fineness (41.67/1000) were to be struck 48 *soldi* of *denari*. As is the case in the mints' documents of the time, the terms *soldi* and *denari* do not have a monetary meaning but a numerical one: that is, *soldi* simply means 12 and *denaro* means 1. Therefore what the document says is that from a pound weight of alloy were to be struck (28 x 12) + (3 x 1) = 339 pieces in the case of the *quattrini* and 48 × 12 = 576 pieces in the case of the *denari*.

On the equivalence between the Pisan pound (weight) and grams see *Tavole di ragguaglio per la riduzione dei pesi e misure che si usano in diversi luoghi del Granducato di Toscana al peso e misura vegliante in Firenze* (Florence, 1782), p. 369, and C. Violante, *Economia, società, istituzioni a Pisa nel Medioevo* (Bari, 1980), p. 214, n. 56.

[18]De la Roncière, *Florence*, vol. 4, p. 118, n. 100.

point the Florentines had obviously convinced themselves that the *quattrino* could not be saved. The commission worked with remarkable speed, and before the
end of the month the monetary authorities of Florence
were able to act. They strengthened the measures designed to discourage the introduction and spending of
the foreign "bad money" in Florence. That was the
ritual. On a more substantive level, they made provisions for the devaluation of the *quattrino* and subse-
quently the *denaro*.

The current *quattrino* contained 0.178 grams of pure
silver. At first, the authorities considered reducing it to
0.151 grams, but then they decided to issue it at parity
with the Pisan *quattrino*, so its silver content was reduced to 0.146 grams. This meant a reduction of 18
percent. For the *denaro*, which had already been devalued in 1366, a much smaller reduction was considered
sufficient, and the content was lowered from 0.0337 to
0.0320 grams of pure silver—a reduction of 5 percent.[19]

The accompanying table expresses the theoretical
silver parity (in grams of pure silver) of the Florentine
and Pisan *lire* at the end of 1371 with reference to the
various types of local currency.

	Florentine *lira*	Pisan *lira*	Pisan *lira* below Florentine *lira* by
	(grams of pure silver)		
when paid with *grossi*	10.84	10.56	2.6 percent
when paid with *quattrini*	8.76	8.76	—
when paid with *denari*	7.69	5.90	23.3 percent

[19]Bernocchi, *Le monete*, vol. 3, pp. 164ff. The decision was made in
September 1371 and put into effect on October 2. For the amendment
of the first decision concerning the metallic content of the *quattrino*
see Bernocchi, *Le monete*, vol. 3, p. 164, n. 2.

The difference of a theoretical 23 percent in the value of the *denaro* in the two states was unimportant on account of the coin's marginal role, its high cost of minting, and its high rate of wear. The coins that mattered were the *grosso* and the *quattrino*, and, as far as these denominations were concerned, by the end of 1371 the two monetary systems of Florence and Pisa could be said to be on the same metallic parity.

Looking back at the events discussed in the preceding pages, one must admit that the Florentines' resistance to devalue their currency was obstinate and coherent.[20] If they eventually yielded to the pressure of Gresham's law, it was not because of lack of good will but rather from lack of room to maneuver. They profited to the utmost from what few possibilities they had and put off for five years a retreat that institutional conditions made inevitable. The only unanswered question is why, after protecting the *quattrino* for years, they yielded completely in 1371 and in a single step put this currency on the same foot as its Pisan counterpart when the commission appointed in September had recommended a devaluation, but under the condition that the silver content be somehow kept higher than the parity of the corresponding foreign currency.

II

When one looks at what happened after the devaluation of the *quattrino* in 1371, one must admit that the Florentine authorities were right in their previous re-

---

[20]The statement by M. Becker (*Florence in Transition*, vol. 2 [Baltimore, 1967–1968] vol. 2, p. 114), that "on the vital question of monetary policy the new government followed the lead of the wool guild" and readily depreciated the silver currency, is absolutely untenable.

luctance to touch that coin. As has been shown in the previous pages, the reduction of a coin was normally followed by a rise in its output as speculators rushed to take advantage of the gap between its face value and the value of its reduced metallic content. In 1371, two circumstances contributed to enhance the postdevaluation boom in the minting of the *quattrino*, namely, the extent of the debasement (18 percent) and the popularity of the coin. In fact, after the devaluation of 1371, the market was literally flooded with new *quattrini*.

The striking of the new *quattrini* began on February 7, 1372.[21] Documentation on the minting activity of the period following is incomplete,[22] but those of the mint's registers that survived enable us to calculate that in twenty-one of the thirty-nine months between February 1372 and April 1375, 23,244,575 *quattrini* were coined.[23] It is not unreasonable to suppose that between the beginning of 1372 and the spring of 1375, about forty million *quattrini* were coined.

We have no way of knowing how many *quattrini* were in circulation in Florence before the new issues, and we cannot estimate what percentage of the new

[21]Bernocchi, *Le monete*, vol. 1, p. lxxxii.

[22]See Bernocchi, *Le monete*, vol. 3, p. 253. The "-" sign used by Bernocchi in his tables can be a source of confusion, because it is used indiscriminately to mean that we know no coins were minted, we do not know whether coins were minted or not, and we know that coins were minted but we do not know in what quantity. For the period November 1374–April 1375, we know that *quattrini* and *denari* were minted (Bernocchi, *Le monete*, vol. 1, pp. 186–187), but we do not know in what amount (Bernocchi, *Le monete*, vol. 3, p. 253). For the periods November 1372–April 1373 and November 1373–April 1374, we have no information whatsoever.

[23]The amount of *quattrini* quoted above in the text represented about 40 percent of the value of the total output of the mint during the period in question (Bernocchi, *Le monete*, vol. 1, p. 253).

issues was remintings of old *quattrini*. Furthermore, we do not know how many newly minted *quattrini* left Florence and invaded the neighboring cities as the Pisan *quattrini* had earlier invaded Florence.[24] These gaps in our knowledge make it difficult to assess the significance of the figures just quoted on the issues of the new *quattrini*. But the behavior of the quotation of the florin gives us a glimpse of the market's reaction to the flood of newly debased coins.

Between 1355 and 1372, the quotation had remained practically stable within the range of 65 to 70 *soldi*. In the course of 1373, the lower rates began to move upward, that is, the spread narrowed, clustering around the upper rates. Then, in 1374, the whole spectrum of rates moved upward, and the maxima of the preceding period were surpassed by wide margins. During 1375, the florin was worth between 72 and 77 *soldi*. At that level the rate stabilized, and between 1376 and 1378 the average value was 75 *soldi* with a spread of plus or minus 4 percent.[25]

In 1371, the *quattrino* had been debased by 18 percent and the *denaro* by 5 percent, while the *grosso* had

---

[24]In the autumn of 1371, the Sienese, who had not minted silver currency for twenty years, found they were under pressure from the Pisan and Florentine *denari*. When it was rumored that Florence was about to embark on a debasement of the *denaro* and on a significant debasement of the *quattrino*, the Sienese decided to ban both Pisan and Florentine currency from their territory (Neri di Donato, "Cronaca senese," *Rerum italicarum scriptores*, vol. 15, part 6 [Bologna, 1937], pp. 638 and 643). Bans of this type usually had little effect: the only result Siena obtained was to see its own currency banned in return by Florence (*ibid.*, p. 647). In 1375, Siena was invaded by *quattrini* (*ibid.*, p. 660). The decision made in 1374 by the town of Perugia to mint *quattrini* (G. B. Vermiglioli, *Della zecca e delle monete perugine* [Perugia, 1816], p. 45) may also have been in reaction to an invasion of Florentine and Pisan *quattrini*.

[25]De la Roncière, *Florence*, vol. 4, pp. 550–558.

been devalued by 2.5 percent in 1369. Following these devaluations, the quotation of the florin had moved from an average of 68 *soldi* in 1371–1372 to an average of 75 *soldi* in 1375: an increase in the exchange rate of the florin on the order of 10 percent in a period of more than three years was not dramatic, but it happened after almost twenty years of stability.[26] Moreover, it happened at a time when poor harvests and adverse economic conditions were causing increased unemployment, lower wages, and higher prices of basic necessities.[27] The period of "fat cattle" for the workers was definitely over, and the question of "the value of the florin" became a disturbing factor in the dialectic between the different groups and class interests.

As Gene Brucker has written, the "democratic" regime in Florence "survived for nearly four decades because it had won the allegiance and support of large and important segments of the citizenry."[28] One of the factors that won confidence in the government and gained the support of large segments of the population was the long period of monetary stability. This stability had eliminated a potential seed of discord between the two major groups of the government—that is, the *Arti Maggiori* and the *Arti Minori*. Harmony, however, turned to discord when the value of the florin sud-

[26]Marchionne di Coppo Stefani exaggerates the length of the period of stability. His passage reflects the psychological reaction to the rise after 1371: "throughout a good thirty years the florin had stood at 3 *lire* 6 *soldi* or thereabouts, and now it has risen in seven years to 3 *lire* 16 *soldi* or thereabouts" (Marchionne di Coppo Stefani, "Cronaca fiorentina," *Rerum italicarum scriptores*, vol. 30, part 1 [Cittá di Castello, 1903], rubr. 877).

[27]De la Roncière, *Florence*, vol. 1, pp. 75, 308, 347, 351, 391–392, 495, and *passim*.

[28]G. A. Brucker, *Florentine Politics and Society (1343–1378)* (Princeton, 1962), p. 387.

denly rose in 1373–1375. In the difficult years of 1376–1377, neither the artisans and shopkeepers of the *Arti Minori* nor the mass of wage earners were willing to swallow an increase that they held responsible for the general rise in prices. The masses wanted the continuation of the good old times of the 1350s and the 1360s. Now, struggling to protect his standards of living, "each man took grist to his own mill," as a chronicler remarked.[29] The popular resentment against the florin's rise of 1373–1375 exploded conspicuously in 1378 and 1380 in the Ciompi revolt and the events that followed.

This is not the place to retell the whole story of the uprising.[30] We may simply mention that, having originated in the power struggles among the ruling factions, the whole affair developed into a revolutionary movement when the so-called *popolo minuto* violently entered into the scene and took over the principal role. The *popolo minuto* consisted of laborers who hired themselves for a wage, apprentices, individuals engaged in menial occupations outside the guild structure (such as porters, stevedores, peddlers, and unskilled laborers), and craftsmen who did not possess guild membership although they were *sottoposti* (that is, subject to the discipline) of the wool guild.[31] This varie-

[29]Marchionne di Coppo Stefani, "Cronaca fiorentina," rubr. 877.

[30]For a general view of the uprising, see Brucker's excellent short synthesis, "The Ciompi," in *Florentine Studies: Politics and Society in Renaissance Florence*, N. Rubinstein, ed. (Evanston, 1968), and the bibliography thereof. See also N. Rubinstein, "The Political Regime in Florence after the Tumulto dei Ciompi," *The Journal of Italian History* 2 (1979).

[31]On the meaning of *popolo minuto* see G. A. Brucker, "The Florentine Popolo Minuto and Its Political Role, 1340–1450," in *Violence and Civil Disorder in Italian Cities, 1200–1500*, L. Martines, ed. (Berkeley and Los Angeles, 1972).

gated mass might well have represented some sixty percent of the population of Florence. One of the first actions of the insurgents,[32] on the very same day that they occupied the Palazzo del Podestà (July 21, 1378), was to present a petition "on behalf of the *popolo minuto* of Florence," in which they requested that the quotation of the florin be reduced by decree to 68 *soldi*. The reason for this particular figure is not hard to understand: the quotation of 68 *soldi* represented the modal value of the florin in the happy days of the monetary stability of 1355–1369. Clearly the lower classes wished or hoped to bring back the good times of the "fat cattle" and typically deluded themselves that an official decree was all that was needed to bring about the magic change. Their petition was approved in the People's Council by 154 votes to 20, and in the Council of the Podestà by 130 to 2,[33] but not surprisingly the provision had no practical effect. The forces of the market prevailed, and the florin remained at 75 *soldi*.[34]

The Ciompi fell on September 1, 1378, and a new government was inaugurated, in which the *Arti Minori* retained much power.[35] As noted in Chapter I, the arti-

[32]Cf. N. Rodolico, "Il sistema monetario e le classi sociali nel Medio Evo," *Rivista italiana di sociologia* 8 (1904); M. Bernocchi, *Il sistema monetario fiorentino e le leggi del Governo Popolare del 1378–1382* (Bologna, 1979).

[33]Archivio di Stato, Florence, *Libri Fabarum*, 40, c. 301 and *Provvisioni*, vol. 67, cc. 12–14.

[34]De la Roncière, *Florence*, vol. 4, p. 556.

[35]"Before the Ciompi revolution, the seven greater guilds provided seven members of the Signoria of nine, including the Gonfalonier of Justice. After [the Ciompi revolution] the share of the greater guilds had been reduced to one third of the Signoria and the Colleges. On 1 September it was raised to nearly one half. Even so, the twenty-three guilds plus the two remaining new guilds retained a

sans and shopkeepers of the *Arti Minori* and the laborers
of the *popolo minuto* had a common interest in monetary
matters. Therefore, the political change of September 1,
1378, did not modify the attitude of the administration
regarding the monetary question. The new regime was
as determined as the last to restore the value of the
silver currency to its pre-1371 level. Thus the problem of
the florin came up again for discussion on January 24,
1379. This time, the proposal was less crude than the
one advanced six months earlier in the heat of the revolt. There was no longer any question of imposing an
artificially low quotation by decree; instead, it was
urged that suitable measures be adopted to bring the
florin back to 70 *soldi*—that of 70 *soldi* had been the high-
est quotation the florin had reached in the period 1355–
1369. The supporters of the new proposal, then, were
moderating the demand for deflation and were ready to
accept the maximum rate of the years 1355–1369, rather
than the average. However, the proposal included a
clause that stated that, if by the month of March following the government had not succeeded in bringing
down the florin's rate to 70 *soldi*, it should reduce by
decree the face value of the *quattrino* from 4 *denari* to 3–
1/2.[36] This clause is the first specific denunciation of the

narrow majority, with five members of the Signoria, nine of the
sixteen *Gonfalonieri di compagnia* and seven of the twelve *Buonuomini*.
But even this majority was abolished in January 1379 when the seats
in the Priorate and the Colleges were divided equally between the
greater and lesser guilds, with the Gonfalonierate of Justice rotating
between the two" (Rubinstein, "The Political Regime in Florence," p.
408). However, the regime that lasted from September 1, 1378, to
January 1382 remained "identified with the rule of the lesser guilds"
(*ibid.*, p. 410).

[36]The proposal passed in January 1379 with 189 votes to 90 in the
People's council and with 155 votes to 40 in the Council of the
Podestà; see Archivio di Stato, Florence, *Libri Fabarum*, 40, cc. 320–
321; *Provvisioni* 67, cc. 122–124.

destabilization caused by the debasement of the *quattrino* in 1371. The clause technically echoed the measure requested by the artisans of Florence against the Pisan *quattrini* in 1367, when it was petitioned that the latter be forbidden to circulate in Florence at more than 3 *denari* each. The proposal's aim was clear enough: by reducing the face value of the *quattrino* in terms of the current money of account, the recipient of a price or wage reckoned in that money would receive a greater number of coins in payment. The proposed measure, which would have made sense if applied to the foreign *quattrini*, was practically nonsense when applied to the local *quattrini*, because the latter currency was the key support of the *lira-soldo-denaro* accounting system. It was indeed foolish to ask for a revaluation of the money of account if its base was devalued.

Subsequent events show that the error was recognized. In October 1380, the supporters of deflation returned to the attack with a much more sophisticated proposal that deserves a special place in the history of monetary thought and practice. The florin still stood at 75 *soldi*,[37] and the wish was to reduce it to 70 *soldi*. In order to accomplish this reduction, the government could have debased the gold florin, but such a move was both politically and economically unthinkable and, besides, it would have had inflationary rather than deflationary effects. Nobody wanted to touch the florin. Alternatively, the administration could have withdrawn the silver currency in circulation and substituted for it a heavier currency. But such an operation was both unthinkable and unfeasible: unthinkable because the Florentine Commune did not issue coins on its own; unfeasible because the Commune did not have

[37]De la Roncière, *Florence*, vol. 4, p. 558.

the financial resources to pay for the operation. What the champions of the deflation proposed on October 24, 1380, was also both unorthodox and costly, but it was within the realm of possibility.

Specifically, they proposed that 2,000 florins' worth of *quattrini* be melted down every two months for a period of eight years.[38] The quotation of the florin at that time was at 75 *soldi*,[39] so 2,000 florins were the equivalent of about 450,000 *quattrini*. If 450,000 *quattrini* were melted down every two months for eight consecutive years, the total operation would have entailed the melting of more than 21 million *quattrini*. Whatever the rationale for this figure, it is obvious that the proponents of the motion of October 24 were aware of a relationship between the value of money and its quantity. In fact, by reducing the quantity in circulation, they aimed at pushing the exchange value of the currency above the value of its metallic content, thus changing its nature from full-bodied to token money.[40]

When the proposal of October 24 was put to the vote in the People's Council, it was approved by 167 votes to 82.[41] Two days later the proposal came before the Council of the Podestà, but before it was voted on Benedetto degli Alberti introduced an amendment. Benedetto degli Alberti was a rich banker who in the

---

[38]Rodolico, "Il sistema monetario"; Bernocchi, *Il sistema monetario*, pp. 25–29; Bernocchi, *Le monete* , vol. 1, p. lxxxix, n. 2.

[39]De la Roncière, *Florence*, vol. 4, p. 558.

[40]A similar experiment was tried in Siena in 1375, when the monetary authorities drastically reduced the quantity of petty currency in circulation in order to support its value. See Neri di Donato, "Cronaca senese," p. 660, and Rodolico, "Il sistema monetario."

[41]Archivio di Stato, Florence, *Libri Fabarum*, 40, c. 378; *Provvisioni* 69, c. 160 v.

political maneuvers of the time had joined the popular party. His political ambitions led him to accept the deflationary policies endorsed by the *Arti Minori*, but his good sense and discernment told him that one should not press such policies too far. The substance of his amendment was that the melting of *quattrini* should be suspended when and if the quotation of the florin fell to 70 *soldi* or below. With this amendment the proposal was put to the vote in the Council of the Podestà and passed by 117 to 57.[42] Thus, with February 1381, the demonetization of the *quattrini* began. The data concerning the meltings are as follows:[43]

	Value of melted *quattrini*		Average quotation of the florin	Number of *quattrini* melted
	in florins (a)	in *soldi* (b)	in *soldi* (c)	(d)
February	2,000	146,000	73	438,000
April	2,000	146,000	73	438,000
June	2,000	142,666	71-⅓	428,000
August	2,000	140,666	70-⅓	422,000
October	2,000	142,673	71-⅓	428,020
December	2,000	145,000	72-½	435,000

In the course of 1381, then, about 2,600,000 *quattrini* were melted down. This was no bagatelle, but the

[42]Archivio di Stato, Florence, *Libri Fabarum*, 40, c. 379v.; *Provvisioni* 69, cc. 176–176v.

[43]Data in column (a) are derived from the text of the law; data in column (b) are from Bernocchi, *Il sistema monetario*, pp. 34–35, and Bernocchi, *Le monete*, vol. 1, p. xc; data in column (c) are derived by dividing column (b) by column (a); data in column (d) are derived by multiplying column (b) by the coefficient 3, because by definition 1 *soldo* = 3 *quattrini*.

maneuver did not bring the hoped-for results. In the first seven months the quotation of the florin lost more than two points, falling from 73 *soldi* in February to 70–1/3 *soldi* in August 1381, but in the next four months it rose again and regained most of the ground lost in the previous seven months. In December, the quotation was 72–1/2 *soldi*, as compared with 73 *soldi* of the preceding February. The fall in the quotation in the first seven months is what one would expect; it was within the logic of the melting operation. Rather surprising instead is the rise of the florin in the second half of the year, when large quantities of *quattrini* continued to be withdrawn from the market and melted down. On the basis of the only data at our disposal, it is difficult to explain the paradox. The most likely hypothesis is that there was a reflux of Pisan petty currency, for it is indeed quite natural that the *quattrini* of Pisa (which now had the same metallic content as those of Florence) would flow into Florence, where the exchange value of the *quattrini* against gold was being artificially raised. The lack of monetary sovereignty that had forced the monetary authorities to devalue in 1366 and again in 1368–1371 must have frustrated their efforts to revalue in 1380–1381.

It would be interesting to know what would have happened if the eight-year plan of demonetization of the *quattrini* had been carried out in full, but political events prevented the plan's completion. On January 31, 1382, the government of the *Arti Minori* was overthrown and replaced with a government dominated by the financial oligarchy. On the very day of its inception, the new government—with an urgency clearly proportionate to the importance of the interests at stake—gave the newly created *Balía* the power to revoke and amend the provisions regarding currency that had been approved the previous October. On February 13, 1382, before the melting scheduled for that month could take place, the *Balía* hastily revoked the provision of October 1380 concerning the melting of *quattrini*.[44] Operation *quattrini* was thus abruptly terminated.

[44]Rodolico, "Il sistema monetario"; Bernocchi, *Le monete*, vol. 1, p. xc.

Conclusion

THE FIRST impression the monetary history of Florence in the fourteenth century conveys is one of curious paradox. The Commune's public debt rose from about 50,000 florins in 1303 to about 600,000 florins in 1343, and then to about 1,500,000 florins in 1364, finally reaching approximately 3,000,000 florins in 1400.[1] Surprisingly, this enormous increase in public indebtedness was accompanied by a relatively modest devaluation of the currency. Between 1315 and 1380 the Florentine *lira* depreciated by approximately 30 percent in reference to the silver content of the *grosso* and *quattrino*, and about 40 percent in reference to the silver content of the *denaro*. Given the progressive marginalization of the *denaro* during the period, it is clear that the weighted aver-

[1]B. Barbadoro, *Le finanze della repubblica fiorentina* (Florence, 1929), pp. 507 and 616; M. Becker, *Florence in Transition*, vol. 2 (Baltimore, 1967–1968), p. 152; R. Barducci, "Politica e speculazione finanziaria a Firenze dopo la crisi del primo Trecento (1343–1358)," *Archivio storico italiano* 137 (1979), pp. 185 and 187, n. 49.

age effective devaluation was closer to 30 percent than to 40 percent.

The paradox does not end there. The history of fourteenth-century Florence was punctuated by events of considerable political importance and of significant economic consequence. Florence had to fight wars against the Visconti (1351–1353 and 1369–1370), the war against Pisa (1362–1364) that cost over a million florins, and the war against the Papacy (1375–1378) that cost about two and a half million florins, without counting the material losses consequent on the Papal Interdict. Yet in the monetary history of Florence one finds no trace of these turbulent events. A student of Florentine history who limited himself to the documents of the mint would be under the impression that nothing happened. The currency was debased only twice, and on both occasions the devaluation had purely monetary origins: the gold-silver crisis of 1345–1347 and the invasion of the Pisan currency in 1366–1371.

The explanation of this curious paradox is actually fairly simple. Unlike modern states, medieval Florence did not finance itself by monetary manipulations. The state received revenues from the mint, but these revenues did not consist of the difference between the face value and the intrinsic value of the currency minted. Rather, they originated in the rights of seigniorage— that is, the tax on the minting activity.[2] If and when a

[2]The state profited marginally and indirectly from a devaluation because, first, a devaluation made it profitable for individuals to take metal to the mint, and as the output of the mint increased, so did the revenues from the seigniorage, and, second, a devaluation of petty currency was normally followed by an increase in the quotation of the florin. Because the seigniorage on the gold coins was collected by the Commune in florins, a rise in their quotation meant an appreciation of the revenues in terms of petty currency (see, for example, the

devaluation was decreed, it was not the state that profited from the gap between the face value of the currency and its reduced metallic content; those who profited were citizens in a position to take metal to the
mint. And those who could carry out this operation
were certainly not the craftsmen, laborers, or shopkeepers; they were the great merchants who also
traded in precious metals, and the bankers and money
changers who were able to round up quantities of old
coins to take to the mint for recoinage. These groups
were among those who also profited from a rise in the
quotation of the florin. Since any substantial devaluation was followed by a rise in value of the florin, it
follows that certain groups gained twice from the devaluation of the currency.

Florentine society (like every other society, regard-
less of time or place) was made up of social and economic groups that had everything to gain from a devaluation, and of groups that had everything to lose. The
balance of political power between these groups obviously influenced the direction of the monetary policy
practiced by the Commune. In 1343 Florence saw the
accession to power of groups that were strongly in favor of monetary stability; these groups increased their
influence and weight during the events that followed
the great plague of 1348. The monetary history of Florence between 1343 and 1378 cannot be understood
without taking into account the position of the *Arti
Minori* vis-à-vis the monetary problem, and the role

accounts for the six months May-October 1373 in M. Bernocchi, *Le
monete della repubblica fiorentina*, vol. 1 (Florence, 1974–1978), p.
lxxxv). The Commune paid out salaries in petty currency, so it stood
to gain in the same manner as the entrepreneurs who collected payments in florins and paid their workers in petty currency.

they played in the government of the city-state during that time.

However, one should be careful not to see in the dialectic of conflicting social and economic groups the unique and exclusive explanation of a process that was in reality much more complex. To begin with, the four-teenth century was a period of relative monetary stabil-ity in other states of Northern and Central Italy, which means that at an international level there were general forces working in favor of monetary stability during the period in question.[3] Moreover, one must take care not to regard the Florentine clothiers, bankers, and mer-chants as devilish creatures continuously pushing for devaluation. There were factors of prestige and civic pride involved with the soundness and stability of Flor-entine currency to which even these groups were not entirely insensible. They reacted strongly when faced with the danger of a fall in the quotation of the florin, just as the craftsmen, shopkeepers, and laborers reacted strongly when faced with a rise in the quota-tion of gold currency. But the stability of both the silver currency and the quotation of the florin was something on which the two opposing parties could agree.

In 1368, when the *grosso* needed protection, it was stated emphatically that Florence had benefited in the past from the prestige of its currency and that that prestige had to be preserved in the future: "conveniens quod civitas Florentina sicut olim precipue in monetis aureis et argenteis claruit ita etiam clareat in futurum."[4] In September 1371, when a commission was appointed

[3]Cipolla, *Studi di storia della moneta: i movimenti dei cambi in Italia dal secolo XIII al secolo XV* (Pavia, 1948), pp. 80–90.

[4]Bernocchi, *Le monete*, vol. 1, p. 156.

to study ways and means of halting the invasion of Pisan currency, its members suggested lower metallic parities for the *quattrino* and the *denaro*, but on the condition that those parities remained in some way superior to those of the corresponding coins of neighboring cities: "dummodo sint majoris valoris quam illi qui cuduntur in terris propinquis civitatis Florentie per quinquaginta miliaria vel infra."[5] This was not empty rhetoric. The sources testify that, over the period 1343–1370, the goal of monetary stability offered the different parties grounds for substantial agreement. The affair of the *quattrini* in 1371–1375 and the consequent rise in the quotation of the florin were like the traditional pebble disturbing the calm waters of the pond. But even on that occasion, none of the disputing parties wanted to push things too far. When the *Arti Minori* acted so drastically as to plan the destruction of approximately twenty million *quattrini*, their aim was not to force an arbitrary deflation, but to restore the quotation of the florin to the level that they considered normal and that had prevailed for the preceding twenty years. Similarly, when the *Arti Minori* were pushed aside in January 1382, the mercantile-financial oligarchy that took power hastened to stop the melting of *quattrini* because they feared it might set off a deflation, but they were very careful not to press for an opposite course. Indeed, for nearly ten years, until 1390, the new group in power maintained a monetary stability.

Here there is another paradox: Florentine society, which was characterized by the most intense turbu-

[5]Ch. M. de la Roncière, *Florence centre économique regional au XIVe siècle*, vol. 4 (Aix-en-Provence, 1976), p. 118, n. 100.

lence and the most extreme excesses, showed itself capable of remarkable restraint and exceptional prudence when it came to the question of money.[6]

[6]It must be stressed, however, that also at the political level the regime that took power in January 1382, although fully committed to confine the lesser guilds to a state of permanent inferiority, "acted with moderation and a sense of continuity". See N. Rubinstein, "The Political Regime in Florence after the Tumulto dei Ciompi," *The Journal of Italian History* 2 (1979), pp. 411ff.

Appendix

The data in these tables are derived from M. Bernocchi, *Le monete della repubblica fiorentina*, vol. 3 (Florence, 1974–1978). Dates are those of deliberations. Actual minting normally began a few weeks later.

TABLE A: GROSSO, 1318–1369

Date	Value (soldi) a	Fineness (-/12) b	Fineness (-/1000) c	Number of pieces struck from 1 lb. alloy d	Average theoretical weight of one piece (grams) e	Average theoretical content of pure silver in one piece (grams) f	Number of pieces returned by the mint g	Seignorage $\left(\dfrac{d-g}{d}\right) \times 100$ (percent) h
1318	2.5	11.5/12	958.3/1000	166	2.04	1.96	163	1.81
1345 (August 23)	4	11.5/12	958.3/1000	132	2.57	2.46	?	?
1347 (July 19)	5	11.5/12	958.3/1000	117	2.90	2.78	111.6	4.62
1351 (January 25)	5	11.5/12	958.3/1000	117	2.90	2.78	110	5.98
1351 (April 25)	5	11.5/12	958.3/1000	117	2.90	2.78	110	5.98
1368 (July 15)	2	11.5/12	958.3/1000	300	1.13	1.08	290	3.33
1369 (June 14–15)	5	11.5/12	958.3/1000	120	2.83	2.71	116	3.33

TABLE B: QUATTRINO, 1334–1371

Date	Value (*denari*) a	(-/12) b	Fineness (-/1000) c	Number of pieces struck from 1 lb. alloy d	Average theoretical weight of one piece (grams) e	Average theoretical content of pure silver in one piece (grams) f	Number of pieces returned by the mint g	Seignorage $\left(\frac{d-g}{d}\right) \times 100$ (percent) h
1334 (August)	4	2/12	166.7/1000	261	1.302	0.217	246	5.74
1347 (July 28)	4	2/12	166.7/1000	318	1.068	0.178	297	6.60
1351 (March 13)	4	2/12	166.7/1000	318	1.068	0.178	270	15.09
1371 (December)	4	2/12	166.7/1000	387	0.878	0.146	336	13.18

TABLE C: DENARO, 1315–1371

Date	Value (*denari*) a	(-/12) b	Fineness (-/1000) c	Number of pieces struck from 1 lb. alloy d	Average theoretical weight of one piece (grams) e	Average theoretical content of pure silver in one piece (grams) f	Number of pieces returned by the mint g	Seignorage $\left(\dfrac{d-g}{d}\right) \times 100$ (percent) h
1315–1321	1	1/12	83.3/1000	540	0.6288	0.0524	444	17.77
1366 (June 22)	1	1/12	83.3/1000	840	0.4053	0.0337	660	21.42
1371	1	0.978/12	81.5/1000	864	0.393	0.0320	708	18.05

TABLE D: SILVER CONTENT OF FLORENTINE COINS 1315–1371
AND SILVER EQUIVALENT OF THE FLORENTINE LIRA

Year	Grams of pure silver (1000/1000) theoretically to be found in						Grams of pure silver equivalent to one lira when paid in			Index numbers of the silver equivalent of lira when paid in		
	grosso I	II	III	IV	*quattrini*	*denaro*	*grossi*	*quattrini*	*denari*	*grossi*	*quattrini*	*denari*
1315–1325						0.0524			12.58			100
1318		1.96					15.68			100	100	
1332–1334					0.217			13.02			100	
1345			2.46				12.32			79		
1347				2.78	0.178		11.12	10.68		71	82	
1366						0.0337			8.08			64
1368	1.08						10.84			69		
1369				2.71			10.84			69		
1371					0.146	0.0320		8.76	7.69		67	61

NOTES: *Grosso* I. *Grosso popolino* with face value of 2 *soldi*. *Grosso* II. *Grosso guelfo* with face value of 2½ *soldi*. *Grosso* III. *Grosso guelfo* with face value of 4 *soldi*. *Grosso* IV. *Grosso guelfo* with face value of 5 *soldi*.

Bibliography

Abulafia, D. "Southern Italy and the Florentine Economy: 1265–1370," *The Economic History Review*, ser. 2, vol. 34 (1981).

Ashtor, E. *Les métaux précieux et la balance des payements du proche Orient à la basse époque.* Paris, 1971.

Barbadoro, B. *Le finanze della repubblica fiorentina.* Florence, 1929.

Barducci, R. "Politica e speculazione finanziaria a Firenze dopo la crisi del primo Trecento (1343–1358)." *Archivio storico italiano* 137 (1979).

Bautier, R. H. "L'or et l'argent en Occident de la fin du XIIIe siècle au debut du XIVe siècle." In *Comptes-rendus* of the Académie des inscriptions et belles lettres de Paris (1951).

Becker, M. *Florence in Transition.* 2 vols. Baltimore, 1967–1968.

———. "Problemi della finanza pubblica fiorentina della seconda metà del Trecento e dei primi del Quattrocento." *Archivio storico italiano* 123 (1965).

Becker, M., and Brucker, G. "Una lettera in difesa della dittatura nella Firenze del Trecento." *Archivio storico italiano* 113 (1955).

Berghaus, P. "Umlauf und Nachprägung des Florentiner Guldens Nördlich des Alpen." In *Atti del congresso internazionale di numismatica, Roma, 11–16 settembre 1961.* Rome, 1965.

Bernocchi, M. *Le monete della repubblica fiorentina.* Florence, 1974–1978.

———. *Il sistema monetario fiorentino e le leggi del governo popolare del 1378–1382.* Bologna, 1979.

Biot, E. "Mémoire sur le système monétaire des Chinois." *Journal asiatique,* ser. 3, vol. 4 (1837).

Brucker, G. A. "The Ciompi." In *Florentine Studies: Politics and Society in Renaissance Florence,* edited by N. Rubinstein. Evanston, 1968.

———. *Florentine Politics and Society (1343–1378).* Princeton, 1962.

———. "The Florentine Popolo Minuto and Its Political Role, 1340–1450." In *Violence and Civil Disorder in Italian Cities, 1200–1500,* edited by L. Martines. Berkeley and Los Angeles, 1972.

Casini, B. "Il corso dei cambi tra il fiorino e la moneta di piccioli a Pisa dal 1252 al 1500." In Garzelli, G., Ceccarelli Lemut, M. L., and Casini, B., *Studi sugli strumenti di scambio a Pisa nel Medioevo.* Pisa, 1979.

Catellacci, D. "La pace tra Firenze e Pisa nel 1364." *Archivio storico italiano,* ser. 5, vol. 2 (1888).

Cessi, R. *Problemi monetari veneziani.* Padua, 1937.

Chiappelli, F., ed. *The Dawn of Modern Banking.* New Haven and London, 1979.

Cipolla, C. M. *Money, Prices, and Civilization in the Mediterranean World.* Princeton, 1956.

———. *Studi di storia della moneta: i movimenti dei cambi in Italia dal secolo XII al secolo XV.* Pavia, 1948.

Corazzini, F. *Le lettere edite e inedite di messer Giovanni Boccaccio.* Florence, 1877.

Davidsohn, R. "Blüte und Niedergang der Florentiner Tuchindustrie." *Zeitschrift für der Gesamte Staatswissenschaft* 85 (1928).

de la Roncière, Ch. M. *Florence centre économique régional au XIVe siècle.* Aix-en-Provence, 1976.

———. "Indirect Taxes or 'Gabelles' at Florence in the Fourteenth Century." In *Florentine Studies: Politics and Society in Renaissance Florence,* edited by N. Rubinstein. Evanston, 1968.

———. "La condition des salariés à Florence au XIVe siècle." In *Il Tumulto dei Ciompi,* Florence 1981.

de Mussis, G. "Chronicon Placentinum." In *Rerum italicarum scriptores*, vol. 16.

de Roover, R. *The Rise and Decline of the Medici Bank, 1397–1494*. New York, 1966.

—————. "Gli antecendenti del Banco Mediceo e l'azienda bancaria di messer Vieri di Cambio de' Medici." *Archivio storico italiano* 123 (1965).

Doren, A. *Die Florentine Wollentuchindustrie vom XIV bis zum XVI Jahrhundert: Studien aus der Florentiner Wirtschaftsgeschichte*, vol. 1. Stuttgart, 1901.

Evans, A. "Some coinage systems of the Fourteenth Century." *Journal of Economic and Business History* 3 (1931).

Falsini, A. "Firenze dopo il 1348: le conseguenze della peste nera." *Archivio storico italiano* 129 (1971).

Franke, H. *Geld und Wirtschaft in China unter der Mongolen Herrschaft*. Leipzig, 1949.

Giard, J. B. *Le florin d'or au Baptiste et ses imitations en France au XIVe siècle*. Bibliothèque de l'École des Chartes, 125. Paris, 1967.

Goldthwaite, R. A. *The Building of Renaissance Florence*. Baltimore and London, 1980.

—————. "Italian Bankers in Medieval England." *The Journal of European Economic History* 2 (1973).

Göller, E. *Die Einnahmen der Apostolischen Kammer unter Johann XXII*. Vatikanische Quellen. Paderborn, 1910.

Grierson, P. H. "The Origins of the Grosso and of Gold Coinage in Italy." *Numismaticky Sbornik* 12 (1971–1972).

Herlihy, D. "Pisan coinage and the monetary history of Tuscany, 1150–1250." In *Le zecche minori toscane fino al XIV secolo*. Pistoia, 1967.

—————. "Santa Maria Impruneta: A Rural Commune in the Late Middle Ages." In *Florentine Studies: Politics and Society in Renaissance Florence*, edited by N. Rubinstein. Evanston, 1968.

Homan, B. "La circolazione delle monete d'oro in Ungheria dal X al XIV secolo e la crisi europea dell'oro nel secolo XIV." *Rivista italiana di numismatica*, (1922).

Hoshino, H. "Per la storia dell'arte della lana in Firenze nel Tre e nel Quattrocento: un riesame." *Annuario* of the Istituto giapponese di cultura, 10 (1972–1973).

—————. *L'arte della lana in Firenze nel basso Medioevo*. Florence, 1980.

Ibn Batuta. *The Travels*. 2 vols. Translated by H. A. R. Gibb. Cambridge, England, 1958–1962.

Lane, F. C. "Le vecchie monete di conto veneziane ed il ritorno all'oro." *Atti dell'Istituto veneto di scienze, lettere ed arti* 117 (1958–1959).

Li, Chien-hung. *Sung Yüan Ming Ching-chi shih-lun*. Peking, 1957.

Lionardo, Aretino. *Dell'Historia Fiorentina*. Translated by D. Acciaiuoli, Venice 1561.

Lopez, R. S. *Settecento anni fa: il ritorno all'oro nell'Occidente Duecentesco*. Naples, 1955. Translated and condensed in "Back to Gold, 1252." *The Economic History Review*, ser. 2, vol. 9 (1956).

Luschin von Ebengreuth, A. *Allgemeine Münzkunde und Geldgeschichte des Mittelalters und der Neueren Zeit*. 2 ed. Munich and Berlin, 1926.

Luzzatto, G. "L'oro e l'argento nella politica monetaria veneziana dei secoli XIII–XIV." In *Studi di storia economica veneziana*. Padua, 1954.

Marchionne di Coppo Stefani. "Cronaca fiorentina." In *Rerum italicarum scriptores*, vol. 30, part 1. Cittá di Castello, 1903.

Martines, L., ed. *Violence and Civil Disorder in Italian Cities, 1200–1500*. Berkeley and Los Angeles, 1972.

Meiss, M. *Painting in Florence and Siena after the Black Death*. New York and London, 1951.

Miskimin, H. A. *Money, Prices and Foreign Exchange in Fourteenth-Century France*. New Haven and London, 1963.

Molho, A. *Florentine Public Finances in the Early Renaissance*. Cambridge, England, 1971.

Montanari, G. "La zecca in consulta di stato (1683)." In *Economisti del Cinque e Seicento* , edited by A. Graziani. Bari, 1913.

Mueller, R. C. "The Role of Bank Money in Venice, 1300–1500." *Studi Veneziani* , n.s., 3 (1979).

Neri di Donato. "Cronaca senese." In *Rerum italicarium scriptores*, vol. 15, part 6. Bologna, 1937.

Paoli, C. "Della Signoria di Gualtieri." *Giornale storico degli archivi toscani* 6 (1862).

Papadopoli, N. *Le monete di Venezia*. Venice, 1893–1919.

Pegolotti Balducci, F. *La pratica della mercatura*. Edited by A. Evans, Cambridge, Mass., 1936.

Peng, Hsin-wei. *Chung-kuo huo-pi*. Peking, 1954.

Pinto, G. "Forme di conduzione e rendita fondiaria nel contado fiorentino (secoli XIV e XV): le terre dell'ospedale di San Gallo." In *Studi di storia medievale e moderna per Ernesto Sestan*. Florence, 1980.

―――. *Il libro del Biadaiolo: carestie e annona a Firenze dalla metà del Duecento al 1348*. Florence, 1978.

Prestwich, M. "Italian Merchants in Late Thirteenth and Early Fourteenth Century England." In *The Dawn of Modern Banking*, edited by F. Chiappelli. New Haven and London, 1979.

Promis, D. *Monete della repubblica di Siena*. Turin, 1868.

Rodolico, N. *I Ciompi: una pagina di storia del proletariato operaio*. Florence, 1945.

―――. *Il popolo minuto*. Bologna, 1889.

―――. "Il sistema monetario e le classi sociali nel Medio Evo." *Rivista italiana di sociologia* 8 (1904).

―――. *La democrazia fiorentina nel suo tramonto*. Bologna, 1905.

Rubinstein, N. "The Political Regime in Florence after the Tumulto dei Ciompi." *The Journal of Italian History* 2 (1979).

―――, ed. *Florentine Studies: Politics and Society in Renaissance Florence*. Evanston, 1968.

Salvemini, G. *Magnati e Popolani in Firenze dal 1280 al 1295*. Florence, 1899.

Sapori, A. "Il quaderno dei creditori di Taddeo dell'Antella e Compagni." *Rivista delle biblioteche e degli archivi* , n.s., 3 (1925).

―――. *La crisi delle compagnie mercantili dei Bardi e dei Peruzzi*. Florence, 1926.

―――. "Le compagnie italiane in Inghilterra." In *Studi di storia economica*. Florence, 1955.

―――. "L'interesse del denaro a Firenze." In *Studi di storia economica*. Florence, 1955.

―――. "Pigioni di case e botteghe a Firenze nel Trecento." In *Studi di storia economica*. Florence, 1955.

―――. "Una parentesi ghibellina nella politica guelfa di Firenze." *Rivista delle biblioteche e degli archivi*, n.s., 2 (1924).

104 BIBLIOGRAPHY

Schaefer, K. H. *Die Ausgaben der Apostolischen Kammer unter Johann XXII*. Vatikanische Quellen. Paderborn, 1911.

Silva, P. "Il governo di Pietro Gambacorta in Pisa e le sue relazioni col resto della Toscana e coi Visconti." *Annali della R. Scuola Normale Superiore di Pisa*: classe di filosofia e filologia 23 (1912).

———. "L'ultimo trattato commerciale tra Pisa e Firenze." *Studi storici del Crivellucci* 17 (1909).

Smith, J. M., and Plunkett, F. "Gold Money in Mongol Iran." *Journal of the Economic and Social History of the Orient*, 9 (1968).

Tavole di ragguaglio per la riduzione dei pesi e misure che si usano in diversi luoghi del Granducato di Toscana al peso e misura vegliante in Firenze. Florence, 1782.

Trexler, R. C. *The Spiritual Power: Republican Florence under Interdict*. Studies in Medieval and Reformation Thought, vol. 9. Leiden, 1974.

Trexler, R. *Economic, Political and Religious Effects of the Papal Interdict on Florence, 1376–1378*. Frankfurt, 1964.

Tullock, G. "Paper Money: A Cycle in Cathay." *The Economic History Review*, ser. 2, vol. 9 (1957).

Vermiglioli, G. B. *Della zecca e delle monete perugine*. Perugia, 1816.

Villani, G. *Cronica di Giovanni Villani*. Edited by F. Dragomanni. Florence, 1844–1845.

Villani, M. *Cronica di Matteo Villani*. Edited by F. Dragomanni. Florence, 1846.

Violante, C. *Economia, società, istituzioni a Pisa nel Medioevo*. Bari, 1980.

Waley, D. P. "The Army of the Florentine Republic from the Twelfth to the Fourteenth Century." In *Florentine Studies: Politics and Society in Renaissance Florence*, edited by N. Rubinstein. Evanston, 1968.

Watson, A. M. "Back to Gold and Silver." *The Economic History Review*, ser. 2, vol. 20 (1967).

Yang, Leng-scheng. *Money and Credit in China*. Cambridge, Mass., 1952.

Index

Abulafia, D., 7n
Acciaiuoli, 9, 10
Account, unit of, 17n.46, 21n, 32, 81. *See also Lira a fiorino; Lira di denari piccioli*
Aghlabids, xi
Alberti, Benedetto degli, 82–83
Antellesi, 9, 10
Apostolic Chamber, xiii
Arti Maggiori, 26n.60; in Florentine government, 77, 79–80n.35; and support of florin, 26, 29. *See also* Bankers; Guilds; Merchants
Arti Minori, 26n.61; in Florentine government, 28–29, 32, 51, 77, 79–80, 84, 89–90; and florin, 26, 51, 78, 80; monetary policy of, 51, 80, 83, 89–90, 91; and petty currency, 26, 29, 51, 80; and *quattrino*, 51; strengthening of, 28–29, 51, 58–59. *See also* Artisans; Craftsmen; Guilds; Shopkeepers
Artisans: and economic crisis, 9, 11, 13; and florin, 78, 79–80; paid in petty currency, 23; and *quattrino*, 51, 67–68, 70, 81. See also *Arti Minori*

AU/AR. *See* Exchange ratio between gold and silver
Augustale, xi, xii

Balducci, F. Pegolotti. *See* Pegolotti Balducci
Balía, 84–85
Bankers, Florentine: collapse of, 2, 5, 6–9, 10, 12, 13; and devaluation, 89, 90; in Florentine government, 84–85, 91; guild of, 26n.60; loans to English king by, 6, 7, 8, 11; and money supply, 13; and Pope John XXII, xiii; power of, xiv, 9; and support of florin, 24–25, 26, 89, 90. See also *Arti Maggiori*
Bankruptcy: of Commune of Florence, 2, 4–5, 8, 43; of English king, 6, 7, 8; of Florentine enterprises, 5n.11, 10, 11, 47
Barbadoro, B., 4n
Bardi, 6, 8–9, 10
Bardi conspiracy, 2
Baroncelli, 10
Bautier, R. H., 19n.48
Becker, M., 28n, 61n.37, 74n

105